INDIA BOND OR FREE?
A WORLD PROBLEM

INDIA BOND OR FREE? A WORLD PROBLEM

ANNIE BESANT

GYAN

Published by

Gyan Publishing House
5, Ansari Road
Daryaganj, New Delhi-110002
Phone: 011-47034999, 9811692060
E-mail: books@gyanbooks.com

Distribution Network
gyanbooks.com
India, USA, Canada, UK, Australia

ISBN: 978-93-7014-235-0 (PB)

First Published, 1926

2nd Impression 2025

Printed at: Gyan Press, Delhi.

INDIA BOND OR FREE? A WORLD PROBLEM
Author: ANNIE BESANT

INDIA
BOND OR FREE?

A World Problem

INDIA
BOND OR FREE?

A World Problem

BY

ANNIE BESANT, D.L.

CONTENTS

INTRODUCTION

THE ordinary history of India, as taught in European and North American schools and colleges, reveals a very remarkable phenomenon. British Rule is taken for granted as natural and desirable. In 1914, before the Great War, in a London Hall, speaking on India's demand for Self-Government—formulated by an eminent Indian, once a member of the House of Commons, Dadabhai Naoroji, President of the Indian National Congress in 1906, as Swarāj, Own-Rule, Self-Rule—I said: "The price of India's loyalty is India's Freedom." Some nonsense had been uttered to the effect that India's loyalty to British Rule should be "unconditional," and this I denied. The Government of India Act, 1915, justified this position, for it spoke of laws "on which the allegiance of the subject depends." Great Britain in her own history, in her Magna Carta and her Bill of Rights, as well as by her revolutions in the reigns of Charles I and James II, and her bargainings with the Prince of Orange and his consort Mary, before they were crowned rulers of the land as William and Mary, had clearly laid down and enforced the doctrine that the loyalty of the subject and the right rule of the monarch were correlatives. In the Indian National Congress held in December, 1918, a resolution was unanimously passed, demanding that in the reconstruction following the War, India should be placed on an equality with the Self-Governing Dominions, and from that time onwards the ideal of Home Rule has shone like a star in the Indian firmament, never to set until Home Rule is achieved, as it will be ere long.

In years previous to 1914, many vigorous attacks on the misgovernment of India by Great Britain had been published in England; one by Dadabhai Naoroji himself, a powerful assault on *Un-British Rule in India*; one by the well-known Socialist, H. M. Hyndman, *The Bankruptcy of India*, an unsparing description of the ways in which, to quote Lord Salisbury's terrible image, the lancet (of taxation) should be applied to parts not already "bled white"; one by Keir Hardie, M.P., *India*, basing his plea for India's right to govern herself on well-known and undeniable facts; one, *Prosperous British India*, the ironic title of a powerful book by William Digby. Many other books of the same kind had been issued from the press, but they reached only a limited class of sympathetic readers.

The foundation of the Indian National Congress in 1885, and the great Indians who appealed for justice to India through it in its annual meetings, enabled India to become articulate, and her intelligentsia created there a platform, whence radical reforms could be loudly demanded. At first, they dealt chiefly with details, with bad laws, cruel injustices, partial administration favouring foreigners at the expense of the inhabitants of the country—

the countless evils inseparable from foreign rule. In the second Congress, 1886, Rājā Rāmpāl Singh declared that the Arms Act—denying the right of Indians to carry arms—outweighed all the benefits of British Rule, for it weakened and debased Indian manhood. He declared passionately:

"We cannot be grateful to it for degrading our natures, for systematically crushing out all martial spirit, for converting a race of soldiers and heroes into a timid flock of quill-driving sheep."

The metaphors may be mixed, but the fervor of the sentiment is undeniable.

One of the greatest of Indians—patriotic, wise, well-informed, patient, strong—Gopāla Krishna Gokhalé—said:

"A kind of dwarfing or stunting of the Indian race is going on under the present system. We must live all our life in an atmosphere of inferiority, and the tallest of us must bend, in order that the exigencies of the system may be satisfied. The upward impulse, if I may use such an expression, which every schoolboy at Eton or Harrow may feel, that he may one day be a Gladstone, a Nelson, or a Wellington, and which may draw forth the best efforts of which he is capable, *that* is denied to us. The height to which our manhood is capable of rising can never be reached by us under the present system. The moral elevation which every Self-Governing people feel, cannot be felt by us. Our administrative and military talents must gradually disappear owing to sheer disuse, till at last our lot, as hewers of wood and drawers of water in our own country, is stereotyped."

The higher the character and quality of the man, the deeper, the more keen, is the passion of resentment felt. I shall never forget the sudden indignation which flamed up in Mr. Gokhalé, when a highly placed English official said to him: "Mr. Gokhalé, why do you not come among us?" The answer rang out sharply: "We will *never* come among you until we can come as equals."

This stunting of the race begins with the education of the boy, and continues until he leaves his University. I have known set as a subject for an essay by Indian boys, "The blessings of British Rule." Imagine if, in a public school in England, there were set as a subject for an essay, "The advantages of establishing German Rule in England." Imagine if a young German professor were brought over to England to supersede an experienced English professor in the teaching of English history. I propose to prove in this little book that England found India an educated Nation and has reduced her masses to illiteracy; that England found the Indian people free, prosperous and rich, and has reduced her to terrible poverty. I willingly admit that in the machinery by which she governs, England is very efficient; but she is inefficient in the vital matters on which the welfare of a Nation depends. She is good in railways, posts, secretarial work, but has undermined the virility of Indians, humiliated them in the face of the world, made India into a subject Nation, imposed on her the "intolerable degradation of a foreign yoke" (Mr. Asquith at the beginning of the Great War). These are crimes for which no number of well-managed railways can make amends. Better bullock carts and Freedom than a *train de luxe* with subjection. Even had she given prosperity instead of ghastly poverty, the crime would still be in the destruction of her self-respect, the cramping of her initiative, the stain upon her National honour. Mazzini rightly said: "God has written a line of His thought over the cradle of every people. That is its special mission. It cannot be cancelled; it must be freely developed." India cannot perform her mission to the world while she is a subject Nation. The world is the poorer by the silence imposed on her.

If some Indians do not feel this, it is because they have been educated in schools and colleges subject to a foreign Government, and live in the atmosphere of inferiority whereof Gokhalé spoke. That they *can* live without feeling it, without chafing against it, is the final proof of their denationalization.

Few educated Indians, however, save those who deliberately put their own advantage above their country's good, are now denationalized to such an extent, and in the awakening of India the Societies for religious reform, the Brāhmó Samāj, the Ārya Samāj, the Theosophical Society (the Founders of which landed in Bombay on February 16, 1879) have taken a leading part. The last-named Society, as an organization, has not entered the political field, though it has contributed many strong fighters to it; but it restored to India pride in her glorious Past; it rescued the country from the materialism, which was striking at the heart of India, by reviving the ancient religions which were slowly perishing through the education given in the Government and missionary schools and colleges; the Government ignored religion, and gave an education purely secular; the missionaries attacked the Indian religions, and taught Christianity; by this policy they merely spread materialism, for the lads and young men had no inclination to embrace a new religion, after hearing their own faiths condemned or mocked.

Invasions of foreigners, before the coming of the apparently harmless English traders, chartered as the East India Company, had mostly been followed by their settling down in the country and becoming Indians, or by their retirement from it when peace returned. Such invasions as that of Semiramis of Nineveh in 2034 B.C.; of Rameses II of Egypt in 981 B.C.; of Darius of Persia in the sixth century B.C.; of Alexander of Greece in 327 B.C.: these all returned home again, leaving some traces behind them, such as a temporary tribute, after that of Darius, of gold-dust (worth a million pounds sterling) from Sindh and north-western Panjāb; or as the impress of Greek Art on sculptures and carvings in the north. India's relations with foreign countries were mostly those of peaceful trade and commerce, as with Babylon the Great in 3000 B.C.; as with Egypt, where mummies dating from 2000 B.C. have been found swathed in finest Indian muslin; Hiram of Tyre traded with her 980 B.C., as is shown by the Tamil names, found in the Hebrew Scriptures, of peacocks, spice and other articles. A large and lucrative trade was carried on with Rome, whither embassies were also sent, both before and after the beginning of the Christian Era; the ladies of Rome's Imperial Courts delighted to deck themselves in Indian silks. Pliny complains of the quantity of gold which was poured into India in many ways, while none returned from it; and this same phenomenon was chronicled by the French observer Bernier, only three centuries ago; the same is true of the intervening centuries, for whenever foreign travellers touch her, they record similar stories of her wealth, and of the happiness and freedom of her agricultural workers and of her craftsmen. We may just glance at two instances, from records left by two Chinese travellers. Fa-Hien visited India in the fifth century A.D., and surmounted many perils on his way thither. But when he reached India—where he lived for six years—he found the roads were safe, and robbers did not molest him; in the villages, he said, people went and came as they chose; capital punishment and torture were unknown; but repeated rebellion was penalised by cutting off the right hand. In the seventh century A.D., Hiouen-Tsang visited India and was present at a quinquennial festival held at Prayāg (now Allahabād), lasting for seventy-five days, and at which five lakhs of people (500,000) were present. At this festival King Harsha distributed the unspent wealth accumulated during the preceding five years, keeping intact his military equipment, weapons, horses, etc. A list of the classes receiving gifts is given, but one day may suffice us. The recipients were ten thousand Buddhist monks, and each one received 100 pieces of gold, one pearl, and one cloth.

Agriculture was prosperous, the soil occasionally yielding three crops in a year, and two crops are mentioned as general. The villages were practically self-contained, as we shall see in dealing with them presently, and the continuous wealth of India was created in her villages, and fed her export trade. Before Christ, Megasthenes, a Greek ambassador, gave a glowing account of the Indian civilization, its prosperous villages, the high character of its inhabitants. Twenty-three centuries afterwards, Sir Thomas Munro, before a Committee of the British Houses of Parliament in March and April, 1813, was asked whether he thought that the civilization of the Hindus would be promoted by its contact with British trade, and he gave the following remarkable answer:

"I do not exactly understand what is meant by the 'civilization of the Hindus'. In the higher branches of science, in the knowledge of the theory and practice of good government, and in an education which by banishing prejudice—and superstition—opens the mind to receive instruction of every kind from every quarter, they are much inferior to Europeans. But if a good system of agriculture, unrivalled manufacturing skill, a capacity to produce whatever can contribute to either convenience or luxury, schools established in every village for teaching reading, writing and arithmetic, the general practice of hospitality and charity amongst each other, and, above all, a treatment of the female sex full of confidence, respect and delicacy, are among the signs which denote a civilized people—then the Hindus are not inferior to the nations of Europe; and if civilization is to become an article of trade between the two countries, I am convinced that this country will gain by the import cargo."

This passing notice of village education throws light on the statement of the *Rāmāyana* (Balakandam § V) that in the kingdom of King Dasharātha there was none who could not read and write; it also says that each was "contented with his possessions," for there were no poor. The admirable arrangements of the Village Communities were responsible for this æonian prosperity; Vincent Smith speaks of highly civilized communities which had existed for untold centuries, and mentions sixteen kingdoms between the Himālayas and the Nerbudda river in the seventh century B.C. The important group of literature, called Purānas (ancient) throws brilliant light on the customs and lives of the ancient Āryan people, and before they came down into India, there existed there the highly developed Dravidian civilization in the north-west, north and north-east of India, and in the south, with which they more or less fraternized, after fighting their way thither. The Āryans brought with them their religion, Hinduism, which, after awhile, dominated India.

The Parsī Community was originally formed out of refugees from Persia, seeking an asylum from Muhammadan persecution, and they form a small, but valuable, part of the Indian Nation.

The Muhammadans carved out their right to citizenship in India by the sword; the first invasion was in the eighth century by Arabs, who conquered Sindh, but found a barrier in Rājputāna that they could not cross. In the tenth century (A.D. 986) came the Sultān of Ghazni, who established himself in Peshawar, and his son won Lahore in 1021. Prithvirāj, slain, closed the Hindu Empire of Delhi, in 1193, that had lasted since the Great War, B.C. 3000, related in the *Mahābhārata*. Delhi then became the capital of the Pathān Empire, which endured till 1526; then came, with the same city as capital, the Mughal Empire, which perished, after more than 300 years, in the Sepoy Rebellion against the British in 1857.

Looking back over the millennia during which the above-mentioned invasions and tradings took place, we note that as to Babylon, Nineveh, Egypt, Persia, Greece, Rome, their Empires have passed away, and only in their ruins and in their tombs can something be found telling of their ancient splendour; but India, their contemporary and equal in those days of their greatness, India still lives, and still there stretches before her a Future yet to be written, a Future which, thus whispers Hope, shall be yet more glorious than her Past.

No country, perhaps, needs more than India that very modern method, at once a Science and an Art, that is called "Political Science". Professor Seeley, in his lectures on this subject, struck a new note in the study of History. As he said:

"This Science is not a thing distinct from History, but inseparable from it. To call it a part of History might do some violence to the usage of language, but I may venture to say that History without Political Science is a study incomplete, truncated, as on the other hand Political Science without History is hollow and baseless—or in one word:

History without Political Science has no fruit;
Political Science without History has no root."

Professor Sidgwick, writing a Preface to the published lectures, remarks:

"As regards the general view that these lectures enforce and illustrate—the two-sided doctrine (1) that the right method of studying Political Science is an essentially historical method, and (2) that the right method of studying Political History is to study it as material for Political Science—I think it may be said that this was one of his deepest and most permanent convictions."

Professor Sidgwick rightly points out in his Preface, that "in order to know what England ought to be and do now, they must study what she has been and done in the past". This is pre-eminently true of

India, and this is a truth which Britain has never realized in her dealings with India; and because she has never realized it, she is draining away all India's true life, and is reducing her to a fifth-rate copy of herself. Emerson, with his keen insight, says of the Englishman, that he

"sticks to his own traditions and usages, and, so help him God! he will force his Island bye-laws down the throat of great countries like India, China, Canada, Australia".

This is fatally true, and explains the superficial success and the deep failure of Britain's Government of India. As another American, ex-President Woodrow Wilson, in his valuable work, *The State*, says:

"Each People, each Nation, must live upon the lines of its own experience. Nations are no more capable of borrowing experience than individuals are. The histories of other peoples may furnish us with light, but they cannot furnish us with conditions of action. Every Nation must constantly keep in touch with its Past."

That is the real reason why no foreign Government can be a success over a civilized Nation, nor can it ever be really stable. The two have no common Past. Their roots are struck in different soils; they look at everything from different angles; and the best intentions are constantly misunderstood.

Wrong motives are supplied; distorted vision deludes. Success is only possible when the invader settles down permanently in a conquered land, so that after a long period of friction, the two have created a common Past, and the stranger is assimilated and become a National. He must forget that his ancestors were foreigners and remember only his recent Past. The Normans thus became Britons. "Saxon and Norman and Dane are we!" sang the poet Tennyson, but their common Past is long enough to make them into one Nation.

Britons are good, though often brutal, Colonists where they come into relations with entirely uncivilized tribes, whose Past is so remote as to be forgotten. But they trample with their heavy boots over the sensitive, delicate susceptibilities of an ancient, highly civilized and cultured Nation, such as India. The destruction of India's Village System was the greatest of England's blunders. She has lately tried to create a Local Government in the place of the one she destroyed, but a Local Government on her own lines, an exotic, instead of one on Indian lines; and it has been a tragic failure, except in Bengal, where greater liberty was permitted.

The Decentralization Commission, appointed in a flash of intuition in 1907, fortunately containing one Indian, Romesh Chandra Dutt—the author of *Civilization in Ancient India*—remarked:

"Throughout the greater part of India the Village constitutes the primary territorial unit of Government organization, and from the villages are built up larger administrative entities. . . . (These Villages) formerly possessed a large degree of local autonomy. This autonomy has now disappeared, owing to the establishment of local Civil and Criminal Courts, the present Revenue and Police organization, the increase of communication, the growth of individualism, and the operation of the individual raiyatwari system, which is extending even in the North of India. Nevertheless, the Village still remains the first unit of administration; the principal Village functionaries—the headman, the accountant and the Village watchman—are largely utilised and paid by Government, and there is still a certain amount of common Village feeling and interests."

Written by an Englishman evidently, unconscious that the words "paid by Government" mark the gulf between the English and Indian Village systems. These officials keep the old names, but the old Pañchāyat (Council of Five) was elected by the householders of the village and was responsible to them; now the officers are responsible to Government officials, and their interest lies in pleasing these, not in satisfying their electors, as of old.

The Report advised the establishment of Village Pañchāyats, Sub-District and District Boards, but all these were to be kept "completely under the eye and hand of the District authorities". That spelt their failure.

I commented on this in the stirring days of the first Home Rule agitation:

"It is admitted that the Village communities have disintegrated under British administration, but the Report urges their re-establishment. It seems that some witness doubted 'whether the people are sufficiently advanced in education and independence for any measure of village autonomy'; there speaks the spirit of the bureaucrat. The Villages had been autonomous for thousands of years; invasions, changes of rule, lapse of time, had left them active; a century and a half of British Rule had made them unfit, in this witness's mind, to manage their own affairs. Why this strange deterioration under a Rule supposed to be uplifting? Because, on the Procrustes-bed of Bureaucracy all that did not fit it had to be chopped off; the villages had their own ways, which had served them well, but they were not the Collector's ways, so they were bad. Only Home Rule will re-integrate Village Government."

Swāmi Vivekānanda, whose eloquent voice rang through the United States of America in the nineties of the last century, knew the value of India's Past to India's Future. He said to India:

"Children of India, I am here to speak to you to-day about some practical things, and my object in reminding you about the glories of the Past is simply this. Many times have I been told that looking into the Past only degenerates and leads to nothing, and that we should look to the future. That is true. But out of the Past is built the Future. Look back, therefore, as far as you can; drink deep of the eternal fountains that are behind, and after that, look forward, march forward, and make India brighter, greater, much higher than she ever was. Our ancestors were great. We must recall that. We must learn the elements of our being, the blood that courses in our veins, we must have faith in that blood, and what it did in the Past; and out of that faith, and consciousness of past greatness, we must build an India yet greater than what she has been."

Swāmi Vivekānanda was right.

An accurate knowledge of the Past of a country is necessary for everyone who would understand its Present, and who desires to judge of its Future. The most ancient Past of India cannot be traced in any available history, because those who now are known as the Āryan Hindus of India, or the Indo-Āryans, only came down from Central Asia into Bhāratavarsha, otherwise called Āryavarta—"The land of the Sons of Bharata," or "The land of the Āryans," "The noble people"—at the time of the sinking of Poseidonis, nine millennia before the Christian Era. Ages before, this Mother-Race of the Āryans had dwelt in Central Asia, and it was there that it developed its national characteristics, and sent out four daughter sub-races westward, ere the Mother-Race itself travelled southwards into India.

Sir William Hunter has described Central Asia as the Home of the Āryans, and has stated how these bands of emigrants went out in successive great expeditions.

They had first, it may be well to mention, come

eastwards from the immense Continent of Atlantis, where they had occupied a small portion of the great tract where now the Atlantic Ocean rolls. Of this early exodus "history" has no knowledge, though in that exquisite gem of Chinese literature, entitled *The Classic of Purity*, we are told it was brought from "the City of the Golden Gate," which was the capital of one of the kingdoms of Atlantis. It is possible that archæological research—which has so wonderfully reconstructed for us by its excavations many of the histories which were regarded not long ago as myths and legends—may yet throw light on those far-off journeyings which brought our forefathers, not yet evolved into Āryans, across what is now the African Sahara, across Egypt, into Arabia, where they long remained; and then some families travelled northwards through Mesopotamia, and onwards to the northern area of Central Asia; there they settled for awhile, undergoing many hardships, attacked by the wild tribes surrounding their colony, massacred down to a few survivors more than once, until the type became fixed, and they finally settled down round that White Island, of which mention is made in Hindu literature, and founded round it a mighty city.

Sir William Hunter is, of course, not responsible for the statements in the last paragraph; these are condensed from clairvoyant investigations; but here again archæology is now at work, and many relics of pre-historical arts and crafts have been unearthed in Mesopotamia, and, much to the puzzlement of archæologists, other resurrected articles, closely resembling these, have been discovered in the north-west of India, in Sindh and the Panjāb, linking up the widely separated lands. And an American expedition has now partly uncovered some remains of a huge city, which will, the excavators say, take years to examine. It will be interesting if they have discovered and will presently unbury the " City of the Bridge," described many years ago by patient clairvoyant researches. It was from this city that families were directed into four large and fertile valleys running between the surrounding hills wherein they lived and multiplied through many generations, developing the special qualities which characterise the four great daughter-races, or sub-races, of the Mother-Race, the centre of which remained the White Island with its guardian City, the City of the Bridge. We are not concerned here with its doings, till it is bidden to go southwards, beyond the mighty range of the Himālayas, to find its new home in India, whither we follow it, though we must perforce pass over the stories of the successive waves that rolled southwards, conquered, colonized, settled down in the huge peninsula known to the modern world as India. " That is another story," and is told elsewhere.

To return to what is, at present, generally regarded as the more solid ground on which stood Sir William Hunter, we learn from him that the early emigrants from Central Asia settled along the southern borders of the Mediterranean ; another emigration founded what became the great ancient Empire of Persia ; a modern Parsi writer claims for this an antiquity of 30,000 years B.C. A third emigration travelled still further westwards, and gave birth to the Nations which dwelt on the northern borders of the Mediterranean—the Greeks, Italians, Spanish—and spread northwards, becoming French, Irish and early British; the name of Kelts, under which all these Nations were grouped—with highly developed emotions, artistic, lovers of beauty—has fallen out of modern anthropology, but is a very convenient title. A fourth emigration travelled to northern Europe, as it became habitable, and were the ancestors of the Slav, Teutonic and Scandinavian peoples. Sir Henry Maine points out how these brought with them from their Asian cradle-land the Village System which still existed in India as late as the nineteenth century. In 1816, the East India Company, which had already drained India of much of her wealth and reduced her to a misery unknown to her during the ages of her immemorial Past, gave the last blow to her degradation by destroying her Village System, thereby depriving her of Education—Sir Thomas Monro said, as we have seen, in his evidence before the House of Commons in 1813, that there was "a school in every village," as was natural since every village had its Temple and every Temple its school; the Musalmān Mosque had likewise its school attached to it—thus, with the Education stifling, only for a time, please God, that "ineradicable love of liberty" which was the child of the free institutions of the Village. It will be remembered that De Toqueville, studying Democracy as developed in the United States of America, laid stress on the fact that the strength of the then Colonies in their struggle for Freedom lay in their

"Townships"; he gave to these "the credit for training their citizens in the habit of Self-Government and regarded the existence of these as a guarantee for the safety of their Freedom when it was won". Those self-ruling Townships were the schools of Democracy, and it is worth while to observe that from the earliest contacts of India with the West, foreign travellers always found her a country of self-ruled villages, "little republics," as they were called. Manu, the most ancient of Indian law-givers, living in a remote antiquity, laid down the Village as the first Unit of Government. His ascending stages of larger Units increased by successive multiples in tens—10 villages, 100 villages, 1,000 villages—and each had its own Government. When they were grouped into kingdoms, and when kingdoms were now and again aggregated into empires, the Village still retained its own self-rule as a recognized free unit; when we find, as in the fourth century B.C., City States, they were again ruled, as were the villages, by Councils; when Alexander, invading India in that century, demanded 100 of the leading citizens of such a City State as hostages, he was met by the answer: "How can the city be governed if deprived of its best men?"

In recent times, much investigation has been made, especially by Indians, into what may be called the Middle Past of India, and two books have been translated from their original Samskrit, that throw a flood of light on the organization of India during that period. These are the *Arthāshāstra* of Kautilya, the Chief Minister of the Emperor Chandragupta Maurya, in the fourth century B.C.; the *Shukraniti*, written in the 7th century A.D. These shew at once the perfection of the democratic organization of the people, and the stability of their institutions. Empires were not of long continuance, even though as admirably carried on as that of Ashoka, with his six Viceroys, in the third century B.C. He well describes the then duties of a Ruler, when he carved on one of his famous pillars :

"On the roads I have had banyan trees planted, to give shade to man and beast ; I have had groves of mango-trees planted ; and at every half kos ($1\frac{1}{2}$ miles) I have had wells dug ; rest-houses I have erected ; and numerous watering-places have been prepared here and there for the enjoyment of man and beast."

Again, we find the same great Emperor providing hospitals for men and animals. Eight centuries later, Fa-Hien, the great Chinese traveller who spent six years in India in the fifth century A.D., describes a free hospital :

"Hither come all poor or helpless patients, suffering from all kinds of infirmities. They are well taken care of, and a doctor attends them, food and medicine being supplied according to their wants. Thus they are made quite comfortable, and when they are well they may go away."

The evidences for village organization cannot be challenged, they exist not only in books dealing with political and social science—of which there were,

Kautilya tells us, fourteen schools in his day—but in the records of travellers in the Middle and Late Past. As I wrote, not long ago : "History does not ever contact an India poor, uncivilized, without arts and crafts of a high order. This perennial condition was based on its villages, the foundation of the widespread prosperity of its masses, and the source of its overflowing wealth." The evidences include : inscriptions cut into the stone walls of temples, or on rocks, or engraved on metal plates, numbers of which have been dug up ; old books like the Buddhist *Jātakas*, giving details of the common life of India, of education and other subjects ; allusions in the Upanishats ; descriptions in the great Epics, the *Mahābhārata*, the *Rāmāyana* ; discoveries on which new books have been written by modern Indians, like Dr. Banerjea's *Public Administration in Ancient India*, which was his thesis for the doctorate of the London University ; books like those of Professors Sarkar, Radhakumal and Radhakumud. There is plenty of literature now from which knowledge can be obtained. It must also be remembered that only a century and a decade have passed since the village organization was destroyed in the Madras Presidency. As late as 1830, Sir Charles Metcalfe, with true insight remarked :

"The Village communities are little republics, having nearly everything they can want within themselves, and almost independent of any foreign relations. They seem to last where nothing else lasts. Dynasty after dynasty tumbles down ; revolution succeeds revolution . . . but the Village community remains the same. . . . This union of village communities, each one forming a separate little State in itself, has, I conceive, contributed more than any other cause to the preservation of the peoples of India through all the revolutions and changes which they have suffered, and is in a high degree conducive to their happiness, and to the enjoyment of a great portion of freedom and independence."

Sir Charles Metcalfe, however, exaggerates the instability of the larger Units of Government ; he was probably thinking more of the North of India, exposed to invasion from beyond its borders, than of the South. Take but a single instance of extraordinary stability, the Pāndya Kingdom in the South. In a Madras Government *Manual of Administration*, this Kingdom is mentioned as existing in 2000 B.C. It was a great Tamilian Kingdom, famous for its literature as well as for its trade and commerce, and it endured till 1731 A.D., when its last ruler committed suicide to escape from the wrongs inflicted by the East India Company. I do not think that Europe can show such a sample of stability as this Indian Kingdom existing for *at least* 3,731 years. But the real interest of history does not lie in the achievements of conquerors, or the stability of kingdoms, but in the greatness of their literature and art, in the presence or absence of freedom, prosperity and happiness of their peoples.

In comparing the results of the Rules of Indian Hindus and Muslims, and of Britons over India, we find that from far back into the night of the Past—

where we have finally only Indian literature to guide us, but that of the most wonderful character, implying the existence of a high condition of culture—the masses of the Indian people have been prosperous, free and happy, save during the last hundred and sixty odd years, dating from the time when the East India Company became a ruling power down to the present day.

The masses suffered when barbarian invaders, like the White Huns, swept over a portion of the country, destroying everything in their way, but such invasions were few and local. When Hindu Kings quarrelled, the battles were between them and their soldiers—rulers and soldiers made a separate caste—and they respected the merchants and the villagers, because these were the sources of wealth, and these wars were generally for the extension of territory. We read of a battle going on, and of agriculturalists ploughing within sight of the fighting. The lives of the wealth-producers were sacred. Safe were also places of Education. The great University of Takshashilā (near the modern Rawalpindi) was on the highway between India and Central Asia; between B.C. 521, when the district was annexed by Persia, and A.D. 510, the city passed under the rule of seven different Nations, yet the University was never molested, but carried on peacefully its training of youth, till the White Huns, A.D. 455, totally destroyed it.

The masses suffered also in the rare cases of famine, and when some epidemic swept over the land. But we hear nothing of "recurrent famines," such as have occurred under British Rule, in consequence of the falling into decay of the old channels for irrigation; nor of such extraordinary mortality as occurred in 1918, in the influenza epidemic, when the deaths sprang from 7,803,882 in 1917 to 14,895,800 in 1918, the reason being the ill-nutrition of the masses, causing their low power of resistance to any strain exceeding that of the normal low vitality. In a terrible famine, under his own rule, Lord Curzon, the Viceroy, spoke of the surprise of the Government at the little power of resistance of the people. But should not Governments know the conditions of the people they rule?

I propose to prove in the following pages that British Rule in India is inefficient in the matters that concern the Nation's life; that India is slowly wasting away and will inevitably perish, unless she regains her right to rule herself. Former conquerors have settled down in the land and become Indians, have become good citizens; the British are birds of passage, attracted by the high salaries and power attached to members of "the ruling race," and the pensions attached to the Services. I know there is much cant about England being the trustee for India's welfare, but I also remember the rejoinder to the statement that "Providence had thrown the responsibility for India's Government on the House of Commons," that "the House of Commons had thrown it back upon Providence". I also know that English recruits to the Indian Civil Service fell off after the Reforms of 1919, because they gave a little power to Indians and made young Englishmen feel "insecure," while the stream of recruits rose again when the Lee Commission had added a crore and a quarter of rupees to the burden that Service places on the bowed shoulders of India. I know also that, until Labour became a power in the House of Commons, that House had a beggarly show of empty benches when Indian questions were on the day's agenda. I know also that the English trustee destroyed the Village Industries of their ward, penalising the sale of her calicoes and other woven goods in order to protect the trustee's mill products in Lancashire, and that the trustee grew richer as the ward grew poorer. All this and much more is familiar to me. But even if British Rule had been a success instead of a failure, if it had not destroyed her Village System and thus reduced her from literacy to illiteracy, from prosperity to misery and hunger, I should still claim Self-Rule for India, since to rule itself is the right of every Nation.

My own life in India, since I came to it in 1893 to make it my home, has been devoted to one purpose, to give back to India her ancient Freedom. I had joined the Theosophical Society in 1889, and knew that one of the purposes for which it was intended by the ever-living Rishis—who sent to the western world, as its Founders, Their Messengers H. P. Blavatsky and H. S. Olcott—was the rescue of India from the materialism which was strangling her true life by the revival of ancient philosophical and scientific religions, and, by the placing of India as an equal partner in a great Indo-British Commonwealth, would avert a war of colour, and bind East and West together in a Brotherhood which should usher in an Era of Co-operation and Peace.

Colonel Olcott had revived Buddhism and greatly uplifted Zoroastrianism ; my first task, as he gladly acknowledged, was to perform the same service to Hinduism, and to this I set myself, showing the insufficiency of materialism as an answer to the problems of life, and the immense superiority of Hinduism as a philosophy encasing an all-embracing religion and a science of yoga, which was an open road to the worlds invisible, to the ancient Rishis of India and the East, to the Saints of Christendom, to the Wisdom which included all religions, excluded none.

This note had been struck by Colonel Olcott ever since he had landed in India. In his very first lecture in Bombay, on March 23, 1879, on "The Theosophical Society and its Aims," he spoke of the "majesty and sufficiency of Eastern Scriptures," and made an "appeal to the sentiment of patriotic loyalty to the memory of their forefathers to stand by their old religions". We found patriotism was aroused by pointing to the splendour of Indian religious and poetic literatures, and that "religion must inspire nationality". It was significant that after the Theosophical Convention at Adyar, in 1884, a number of the delegates and members went over to Madras and formed the organizing Committee of the National Congress-to-be, which met in Bombay in 1885, and became the Voice of India ; the National self-respect, aroused by revived pride in Hinduism, leading to the National Ideal of Self-Government.

In his book entitled *Indian Unrest*, Sir Valentine Chirol indignantly wrote :

" The advent of the Theosophists, heralded by Madame Blavatsky and Colonel Olcott, gave a fresh impulse to the revival, and certainly no Hindu has done so much to organize and consolidate the movement as Mrs. Annie Besant, who, in her Central Hindu College at Benares, and her Theosophical Institution at Adyar, near Madras, has openly proclaimed her faith in the superiority of the whole Hindu system to the vaunted civilization of the West. Is it surprising that Hindus should turn their backs upon our civilization, when a European of highly trained intellectual power, and with an extraordinary gift of eloquence, comes and tells them that it is they who possess, and have from all times possessed, the key to supreme wisdom ; that their Gods, their philosophy, their morality, are on a higher plane of thought than the West has ever reached ? "

It soon became clear that in addition to reclaiming adults to their ancestral faiths, it was absolutely necessary to start a system of National Education, which would include religion. Already Colonel Olcott had changed the face of Ceylon by making Education the handmaid of Buddhism, and covering the Island with numbers of village schools in which the children learned their ancestral faith. Zoroastrianism had its own schools, for the Parsis were a wealthy though a small community ; no Parsi grew up outside his religion. The Muhammadans had established a fine School and College at Aligarh, and had many schools scattered about the country. Hindus awoke to the fact that in losing their ancestral Faith they were also losing their Nationality, no longer recalling in their daily prayers their seven sacred cities from Kedarnāth in the Himālayas to Rāmeshvaram on India's southernmost border, nor visiting them and her sacred watering-places on pilgrimages, making all India one Holy Land to every Hindu. As a result of the religious awakening, an enthusiastic group of Hindus in Benares opened the two upper classes of a High School and the two lower classes of a College, subscribing the necessary funds and forming a Managing Committee, in 1898. This became famous as the Central Hindu School and College, and in 1916 it became the nucleus of, and presented its lands, buildings and funds to, the present Hindu University. The Governor of the United Provinces, Sir Antony Macdonnell, denounced it as "seditious," but we went quietly on, and so justified ourselves by our work that the Prince and Princess of Wales—now King-Emperor and Queen-Empress of India—visited the College when in India, and their son, the present Prince of Wales, accepted the first Doctorate of the Hindu University, its heir and successor. Colonel Olcott, President-Founder of the Theosophical Society, writing on the relation between the National religion and Nationality, remarked: "This has been the keynote of all our teaching in Asia from the very commencement, and the creation of the Central Hindu College at Benares by Mrs. Annie Besant has been made possible thereby."

Colonel Olcott's own work in Madras for the outcastes, born from his passionate sympathy for their sufferings and his American hatred for their oppression, led him to establish in 1894, his first free school for outcaste boys and girls. He started five of these in Madras, and they flourished exceedingly. His work for Buddhist Schools in Ceylon has already been mentioned.

In the Past, Education divorced from Religion was unknown, as we shall see in dealing with Education. The Ārya Samāj, a reforming Hindu Society, had taken up educational work at Lahore, and had a College in which their tenets were taught, and the Muhammadans, as just said, had erected a first-rate College and School at Aligarh; this also, later, like the Hindu College and School, blossomed into a University and is now the Muslim University. These with the Colleges and Schools under the Theosophical Trust, all make religion an essential part of their curricula. The last-named differs from the others in that its institutions teach groups of students their own religions, and all join each morning in a Common Act of Worship, in which a teacher or a student of each religion represented in the institution recites a well-known prayer of his own faith, all standing reverently through the whole. The service generally concludes with a patriotic song, such as "Vande Matāram," or one written by Dr. Rabindranath Tagore. It is found that this reverent recognition of the great religions has an admirable result in the friendliness of teachers and students and, together with the total abolition of beating and all similar brutalities, refines the lads, makes them fearless, happy and self-disciplined, as all boys should be. The Scout Movement contributes much to this result, and games and athletics keep the body strong, healthy and alert. The boys—and the same is true of the girls—grow up naturally into good citizens, patriotic, loving their own country, but not hating or distrusting other lands.

We shall deal in this book with the Awakening of India from the drugged sleep which followed the Battle of Plassey, in 1757, to the Sepoy War which broke out a century later, after which the East India Company disappeared, and the Queen of England became the Empress of India. The changes were at first slow, then more rapid, until the claim was made for Home Rule in 1906, and was never again silent.

In 1917, having carried on a vigorous propaganda for Self-Government for three years in a weekly and then a daily journal, with securities imposed and duly forfeited, and having vainly—though it roused public opinion—fought out the question of the political liberty of the Press in the Madras High Court, the Government of Madras interned two of my colleagues and myself, and raised a storm of indignation that caused the superior Government to interfere to set us free, and caused me to receive the highest honour the subject Nation could give, the Presidency of the only Parliament it had, its National Congress. In that Congress I voiced the feeling which had awakened and which now animates all patriotic Indians with ever-increasing force; for though the War has been over for more than seven years, and India fought for

Britain in every theatre of that War, India is not yet free. I wrote:

"It is not a question whether the rule is good or bad. German efficiency in Germany is far greater than English efficiency in England; the Germans were better fed, had more amusements and leisure, less crushing poverty than the English. But would any Englishman therefore desire to see Germans occupying all the highest positions in England? Why not? Because the righteous self-respect and dignity of the free man revolt against foreign domination, however superior. As Mr. Asquith said at the beginning of the War, such a condition was 'inconceivable, and would be intolerable.' Why, then, is it the one conceivable system here in India? Why is it not felt by all Indians to be intolerable? It is because it has become a habit, bred in us from childhood, to regard the Sahab-log (English) as our natural superiors, and the greatest injury British Rule has done to Indians is to deprive them of the natural instinct born in all free peoples, the feeling of an inherent right to Self-Determination, to be themselves. Indian dress, Indian food, Indian ways, Indian customs, are all looked on as second-rate; Indian mother-tongue and Indian literature cannot make an 'educated' man. Indians as well as Englishmen take it for granted that the natural rights of every Nation do not belong to them; they claim a 'larger share in the Government of the country,' instead of claiming the Government of their own country, and they are expected to feel grateful for 'boons,' for concessions. Britain is to say what she will give. The whole thing is wrong, topsy-turvy, irrational. Thank God that India's eyes are opening ; that myriads of her people realise that they are men, with a man's right to manage his own affairs. India is no longer on her knees for ' boons ' ; she is on her feet for Rights. It is because I have taught this that I am President of this Congress to-day.

"This may seem strong language, because the plain truth is not usually put in India. But this is what every Briton feels in Britain for his own country, and what every Indian should feel in India for his. This is the Freedom for which the Allies are fighting ; this is Democracy, the Spirit of the Age. And this is what every true Briton will feel is India's Right, the moment India claims it for herself, as she is claiming it now. When this right is granted, then will the tie between India and Great Britain become a golden link of mutual love and service, and the iron chain of a foreign yoke will fall away. We shall live and work side by side, with no sense of distrust and dislike, working as brothers for common ends. And from that union shall arise the mightiest Empire, or rather Commonwealth, that the world has ever known, a Commonwealth that, in God's good time, shall put an end to War."

I

THE INDIAN VILLAGE

A.—Its Past

THE immemorial existence of the Indian Village, the Laws laid down for its main arrangements, its officials, its servants, its general inhabitants, its self-contained character, all this is a matter of common and unchallenged knowledge.

The first thing to notice in the Indian Village is that it was always self-governed in the Past. The Village Council was the Pañchāyat, presumably so-called because, when villages were not large, a Council of five (panch) persons sufficed. Putting aside China, for lack of full information, we have in India the most accessible material for reconstructing the free civilisation which in the West was crushed by feudalism. Sir Henry Maine, in his *Village Communities*, points to this fact, and remarks (p. 122) that the Village Council " is always viewed as a representative body and not as a body possessing inherent authority," and he speaks of its "essentially representative character". It is interesting to note that in India, uneducated people still elect by one of the methods described in old inscriptions as those used in electing village Councils. To Maine, the interest of the Indian Village chiefly consisted in the fact that he found living there institutions for the traces of which in the West he was laboriously seeking.

"The Indian Village Community is a living and not a dead institution. . . Over the greatest part of the country the Village Community has not been absorbed in any larger collection of men, or lost in a territorial area of wider extent. For fiscal and legal purpose it is the proprietary unit of large and populous Provinces." (Lecture I, p. 13.)

India presents three layers of races—Kolarian, Dravidian and Āryan. The first is represented by Santals, Bhils and other aboriginal tribes, and need not detain us. The Dravidians, as already mentioned, were the population of the South chiefly, and were highly civilized; they were, also, as noted in the Introduction, spread over the north-east, north and north-west. Their civilization was less free than that of the Āryans, for their Central Governments appointed the headmen of the villages, in this resembling the English, thousands of years later. They also set apart a portion of the village land to be cultivated by the villagers for the Government, and the crops of this were the only tax.

The Āryans bring the self-contained Village, the "little republics" of which Megasthenes speaks, and they elected their own headmen. These villages might or might not form themselves into groups; as mentioned in the Introduction, Manu's *Institutes* speak of groups of 10, 100, 1,000 (§ 115-117), in which the 1,000 villages formed a province (desha). Varieties of Government arose in these increasing areas, in the kingdoms formed of provinces, and the empires formed of aggregations of kingdoms. In the early provinces, the ruler was expected to visit each village each year to administer justice in inter-village disputes ; but he did not interfere in other local matters. This comes out well in the case of a King's mistress, who wanted to share his power ; he answered : " My love, I have no power over the subjects of my kingdom ; I am not their lord and master. I have only jurisdiction over those who revolt and do wrong." (Quoted in Lord Ronaldshay's *India : A Bird's Eye View*, pp. 137, 138.) The good citizen lived without fear of the King, who was essentially a Protector.

The annual visits, of course, became impossible as kingdoms increased in size, but a King had always a Council, and Ministers or other officials shared his duties. " A King without a Council," said Kautilya, " is like a cart with one wheel."

To return to the self-contained Village, a unit of that Village System, peculiarly Āryan, as Sir Henry Maine shows, since they carried it with them in their emigrations and planted it all over Europe. They naturally also brought it with them, when they came down into India and settled there. We never find Āryan or even Dravidian India without Village Self-Government, though, as just said, the Dravidian was less free ; it was the source, the cause, of the unique prosperity which continued for ages, but which finally led to her enslavement, as it attracted to her the hordes of European merchants, who fought on her soil, lured Indian Kings into their quarrels, played off one against the other, and finally reduced them to practical vassalage—as we have seen to-day—despite the treaties which were supposed to safeguard their power.

We never, then, find Āryan India without her Village System, of which the election of all officials was an essential part; the Village is always an organized community, organized for independent self-existence, containing the necessary elements for a full and satisfactory social life, educated and cultured.

The first thing to observe is that the village owned the land on which it lived and worked. There were always at least three buildings, that may be called public institutions, needed in every village: the Temple, with its tank, where the villagers worshipped; the School, where their children were educated; the Rest-house, where travellers were entertained. The remainder of the inhabited part of the land was occupied by the house-sites of the villagers, the roads and open spaces. The laws secured to every family its house-site, with a yard and a vegetable garden; the householder was enjoined to plant flowers outside his house on the left side, and flowering trees were to line the roads or be planted "very near" the village; a list of fruit-bearing trees is given, and directions for manuring them. Outside all the buildings, ringing them round, was the arable land for the food supply; round this again pasture-land for the flocks and herds; Manu's *Institutes* directs that round small villages a ring 400 cubits wide, and round large villages one of 1,200 cubits wide should be pasture.

Beyond that came the forest, either natural, if the village had been built in a clearing, or made by the planting of wild trees, timber-trees and others yielding wood wanted for necessary purposes, for carpenter's work, or manufactures.

We also read in the *Arthāshāstra* of the construction of new villages:

" . . . Either by inducing foreigners to immigrate or by causing thickly populated centres of his own kingdom to send forth the excessive population, the King may construct villages, either on new sites or on old ruins." (Book II, Chap. I, p. 51.)

Mr. John Matthai (*Village Government in British India*) tells us of such a case in the thirteenth century, A.D.:

" A similar instance of a King taking the initiative in the formation of a village community appears in a South Indian inscription of the thirteenth century, A.D. The village in question was intended to accommodate 108 Brahmans. Sufficient land was purchased for the village site, which was to contain room for the erection of a temple, and for the house-sites of the 108 Brahmans, of the village servants, and of the men in charge of the village library (Sarasvati-Bhandharattar). The lands were bought from the old title-holders and tenants, with all the benefits and appurtenances which belonged to them; and these were transferred in their entirety to the new settlers. A right of way was secured over certain lands outside the village for the Brahmans to walk to the tank for the performance of their daily prayers (Sandhyavandana). Land was also provided for grazing cattle, for the maintenance of the families of the new settlers, each of whom appears to have received a definite piece of land, and for the remuneration of the village officers and artisans." (Chap. I, p. 12.)

Kautilya lays it down as a general principle that it is the duty of the King to unite families into villages. He writes :

" Villages consisting each of not less than a hundred families, and of not more than 500 families of agricultural people of the Shudra caste, with boundaries extending as far as a krosha or two (a krosha or kos was three miles), and capable of protecting each other, shall be formed. Boundaries shall be denoted by a river, a mountain, forests, bulbous plants, caves, artificial buildings or by trees." (Book II, para. 46.)

Directions are given for fortified buildings of different kinds, according as the centres formed were of 10, 200, 400 and 800 villages. The distribution of the population of a State was evidently regarded as one of the duties of the Ruler ; it should not be allowed to become congested in any place.

Instructions for the building of such Villages are given in the *Manasara Shilpashāstra*. (The word *Shāstra* denotes a Scripture or other book having authority, and it may deal with any subject, " sacred or profane " as divided in the West. We do not find that sharp division in the East.) *Shilpa* denotes Arts and Crafts. The Brāhmana had his Shāstras—Bibles—dealing with religion, philosophy, metaphysics, science, yoga, with all comprised within the "Brāhmavidyā," the Science of Brahman, the Universal, Omnipresent Life. This Science has two divisions: the Higher, "the direct knowledge of Him by whom all else is known"—that, a man must find for himself; the Lower, headed by the Vedas, including all that one person can teach to another. Every profession, every art, every craft, statesmanship, and politics had therefore its Shāstra; hence the craftsman had his, for his craft was also a manifestation of the Divine Life: naught can be excluded from the Universal.

Returning from this digression, necessary to explain the fundamental basis of all life and all institutions in India, I note that Mr. Matthai mentions the reappearance of such artificial manufactured Villages, as they may be called, in the "Canal Colonies of the Panjāb," in the "Chinab Canal area". He refers us to Mr. B. H. Baden-Powell's work, *The Indian Village Community*, and tells us how "colonies of peasant land-holders are encouraged to migrate from congested areas and to form 'artificial villages of peasant lessees,' raiyatwari villages as they are now called". (See *loc. cit*, p. 445.) One may imagine that the British even are falling under the old spell of India, when we see the artificial villages of the fourth century B.C., and of the thirteenth century A.D., reappearing in the twentieth century A.D.

Many lists of village officials and servants are

found, relating especially to the South of India, where the Madras Government has done most useful work in encouraging Indian scholars in research work, and in publishing inscriptions found on rocks and walls, and on metal plates dug up. The Report of a Select Committee of the House of Commons, Parliamentary Paper, 1812, gives a list: Headman; Accountant; Watchman; Boundary-man; Superintendent of Tanks and Watercourses; Brāhmana, the Priest; Schoolmaster; Astrologer; Washerman; Barber; Smith; Carpenter; Potter; Cow-keeper; Doctor; Dancing Girl; Musician; Poet. One or more weavers, a number of looms, and workers at other crafts, stone-masons, gold-smiths, copper-smiths, and others are also mentioned in other lists. On the whole, we find well-organized communities, providing their necessaries within their own limits. These officers and servants were all paid by "shares" in the village lands, or by stated shares in the village crops. Gifts to them were sometimes made at festivals. Their services were rendered free, as needed by each household. Here are two copperplate records from the sixteenth century A.D., when there was a migration which restored a ruined village; they may serve as samples:

"To the office of Ironsmith—to the westward a dry field of black soil, in which two tums of grain may be sown; also a field of wet land, watered by the channel, in which two tums of grain may be sown.

"To the Office of Carpenter—to the north a dry field of black soil, in which two tums may be sown;

also a field of wet land, watered by the channel, in which two tums may be sown."

The Ironsmith in this case was Daggoji and the Carpenter was Nagoji. I am sure that these respectable artificers never thought that their names would be recorded in the twentieth century by a white woman, an admirer of their old arrangements.

Very interesting light is thrown on the constituents of a large and well-organized Temple community—a village in itself—by an account of the contributions made by villages under a Chola King, between A.D. 985 and 1013, to the building and provision for the great Temple at Tanjore. The members of the Village Assemblies were ordered to supply specified persons or articles. The details are all given in the *South Indian Inscriptions* (Vol. II, pp. 278-333): 145 Village Assemblies were ordered to supply Brāhmanas, Temple treasurers, Brāhmacharis, Temple servants and Temple accountants; 114 Village Assemblies were ordered to supply watchmen. The allowances to these were to be paid out of the revenue owing to the King. Others had to supply articles required for the Temple worship; the King himself provided no less than 400 dancing girls for the services in the Temple; each was given a house and a share of land. Six dancing masters were given two shares each. An accountant, a fortune-teller, persons to recite in Samskrit and Tamil, singers, musicians, pipers, drummers, a potter, a barber, a washerman, a tailor, a brazier, a carpenter, a goldsmith, are all provided with land for their support. There were more than one in each of these classes, and each had his own share.

It helps one to realise the wealth of the villagers when such indents could be made on them, and when the maintenance of these Temple officials and servants could be paid, year after year, out of the revenue paid to the King. This was a share of the crops, paid to him for his protection, and varied from a fourth to a twelfth in different parts of India. Amusements were provided for, and the Temple with its processions, in which the dancing girls played (and still play) a great part, with the musicians, the pipers and drummers and singers; the recitations in Samskrit and Tamil; the visits of pilgrims; the daily services—all these made up the pleasures of Village life; nor must we forget the games, the wrestling, the lathi-play, the dagger-play, the clubs, and athletics generally. The village girls also had various dances, which may still be seen in girls' schools. It has often been said that, in India, education and culture spread from the forest to the villages, with their varied trades, the rich products of their looms, with their recitations and bhajana (hymn-singing) parties. The restoration of the Village life would mean the restored gaiety, the happiness of the masses of the people.

I have said that the land belonged to the Village, and this common right was secured by periodical re-allocations of the cultivable land among the cultivators; in other cases, the land was cultivated in common and the produce was divided. The pasture land was in common; every villager could graze his animals thereon, under the care of one or more cow-keepers and shepherds; all could cut wood for house-building, fuel, etc., from the surrounding forest, and gather leaves, etc., for manure. All watering-places—river channels, ponds, etc.—were free to all. All lands which were tax-free were common. In some villages, where there were many persons of one occupation, quarters (cheri) were assigned to those similarly engaged; there would be a carpenters' cheri, a washermen's cheri, and so on. As many falsehoods are told of the oppression exercised by the caste people over the non-caste, or Pañchamas, I may quote from the records examined by Dewan Bahadur T. Rangachari (now a member of the Indian Legislative Assembly), from whose useful compendium many of these facts are quoted:

> "There will be a Kovil, or small Temple for the Pañchamas, free homesteads, free grazing-ground, small plots of land set apart for their use, right to cut jungle-wood for fuel or take jungle-produce for manure, right to take jungle-timber for house-buildings, and generally all the claims which the labouring population has in other villages."

Village Councils.

A Village was governed by a Council; in a small Village, with a less developed population, all the adult men formed a Council; in the larger, the Council was elected, and women are sometimes included in it. In the Madras Annual *Epigraphical Reports*, we find detailed information. From these I summarise one example, taken from the inscriptions cut into a temple wall in A.D. 918, 919, 920, 921. Six Committees were to be elected ; Annual, Tank, Garden, Supervision of Justice (this included a woman), Gold and Pancha Varna. Qualifications of voters are laid down, and the method of election. The village was evidently large, as it had 30 wards. The names of the qualified electors in a ward were written on tickets and tied together. The thirty bundles were placed in a pot. A general assembly was called, and a young boy plunged his head into the pot and took out a bundle. This was put in another pot and shaken loose. The boy again put his head into the second pot, took out a ticket and placed it in the hand of the officer, " who shall receive it on the palm of his hand with the five fingers open " ; he reads out the name and the man is elected. Thirty men are chosen in this way, 12 of these, who had served on the Garden and Tank Committees, or were advanced in learning and age, were placed on the Annual Committee ; 12 were placed on the Garden and 6 on the Tank Committee, chosen by, " Karai katti "—apparently oral voting, like the " Aye " and " Nay " of Parliament when " the Question is put ". But the rule here was that there must be unanimity of votes, and Mr. Matthai tells us (*loc. cit.*, p. 30) that an inscription of the ninth century, Tinnevelly, lays down the rule : " Members should, in no case, persistently oppose by saying 'nay, nay' to every proposal brought before the Assembly." Such a persistent non-co-operator was fined. Other ways of voting were by coloured slips of wood, representing "Aye" and "Nay," either given to the officer openly, or thrown secretly into a box. The Buddhist Sangha, in its local assemblies, used the latter method, and it may be remembered that the Lord Buddha organized His Sangha on the model of the Councils of His time.

The laws administered by the Village Councils were for the most part customary. They must have occasionally needed to provide new rules for new circumstances that arose, and in that sense they were legislative bodies. But their duties were chiefly administrative—the distribution of water, the upkeep of roads, the seeing that the villagers performed their rightful share of the general work necessary for the upkeep and welfare of the Village.

Where the common good was concerned, free labour was readily given by the villagers, and an important part of the Village Council's work was directed to the planning and supervision of such necessary tasks. The laying out and repairs of roads, the digging of tanks and wells and water-channels, the erection of public buildings, were carried out by this co-operative free labor. So also the cultivation of lands assigned to any superior authority as payment for its protection came within the work performed by the villagers without payment. Some Indian States, such as Mysore, keep up this ancient custom, but in Mysore the value of the labor thus given is calculated and a grant almost equal to its value is made by the State. Rupees 44,978 were thus earned by a Village in a recent year.

Mr. C. P. Ramaswami Aiyar (now the Hon. Sir C. P. Ramaswami Aiyar, K.C.I.E., Vice-President of the Executive Council of the Government of Madras), says in a valuable pamphlet on *Co-operative Societies and Pañchāyats* :

" In Kautilya's *Arthāshāstra*, Book III, Vol. 10, villagers are contemplated as constructing and maintaining in their corporate capacity works of public utility ; and Professor Rhys Davids says : ' Villagers are described in the Buddhist books as uniting all their care to build mohallas and rest-houses, to mend the roads between their own and adjacent villages and even to lay out parks.' (*Vide* P. Banerjea's *Public Administration in Ancient India*, p. 293, note 2.) In Mysore, now, in many districts the villagers give half a day's work free, per week, for works of public utility, and the aggregate value of the work done is astounding. Every village in the times of the *Arthāshāstra* (fourth century B.C.) formed an integral part of the general administrative system, and the Village was the foundation of the Governmental edifice. The Village Government of those days partook not only of the administration of the executive, but also of judiciary, functions, as will appear from the Ceylon inscriptions dealing with the administration of criminal justice of communal courts. To the credit of the Madras Government, it must be said that, as against Sir T. Munro, who was a thorough individualist, the Madras Board of Revenue desired in the early years of the last century to leave the authority of the Village institutions unimpaired. But

Sir Thomas Munro had his way, and the Village Communities lost their vitality."

The Mysore Administrative Report states:

"The Village Communities continued to evince much interest in this work, and many works of public utility, such as construction of school buildings, sinking wells and opening roads, clearing lantans and planting trees, were carried out through their exertions throughout the State."

In the *Report of the Indian Irrigation Commission,* quoted by Mr. Matthai, it is stated that in the Madras Presidency such works irrigate "collectively an area equal to that irrigated by all the larger works which have been constructed by the British Government". Inscriptions show that both Hindu and Musalmān Rulers considered that one of their main duties was the making of large reservoirs and water-courses, while the villagers made the connecting channels and tanks for their own village. Some of the great works made in the Tanjore District in the tenth century A.D. have been allowed to fall into decay, with the result of recurrent famines when the rainfall fails.

We shall refer to the village schools and their disappearance when we study Education as it was, before the Village Councils were destroyed.

The Village Council also possessed civil and criminal jurisdiction within its own boundaries. I have already mentioned the Committee of Justice. One inscription tells of action taken by it against a woman who refused the payment of a tax in the eleventh century. Another, in the following century, tells of a man who was sentenced to keep a lamp burning in the Village Temple for having accidentally shot a man "not belonging to his own Village"—evidently a much lesser crime than shooting one belonging to his own community. The English principle that a "man should be tried by his peers" seems to have been carried out very exactly, as we read that a fisherman should be tried by fishermen, a hunter by hunters.

Mr. Matthai remarks on the great utility of this local justice. He says:

"The chief advantage of a Pañchāyat was, of course, the obligation which the very nature of the tribunal threw upon parties and witnesses to tell the truth. In a small concentrated community, it was not likely that any one who cared to live a comfortable life would venture an untruth before a council of his fellows. Sleeman, in his *Rambles and Recollections* (Vol. II, pp. 34, 35), has an interesting comment on the difficulty he sometimes felt in arriving at the truth in cases in which sepoys were involved, 'and yet, I believe, there are no people in the world from whom it is more easy to get it in their own village communities, where they state it before their relations, elders and neighbours, whose esteem is necessary to happiness, and can be obtained only by adherence to truth.' Another advantage which must have helped the long continuance of the system was that in the greater or lesser degree of isolation in which village communities often found themselves, there was no other tribunal of any competence before which disputes could be easily lodged. Moreover, the local authority and knowledge of the elders rendered the Pañchāyat in ordinary cases—that is in cases which did not entail undue labor—'clear and prompt in its decisions.' "

Mr. Matthai quotes Mr. A. D. Campbell, I.C.S. (Indian Civil Service) as saying :

" I have often found the parties (disputes on land revenues) resist all argument on the part of my native servants as well as of myself, but immediately concede the point with cheerfulness when decided in favour of the Government by a Pañchāyat."

The habit of obedience of a Pañchāyat is in the blood of the people. No Local Government can be successful that does not rest on the Village Pañchāyat as its foundation.

Another important duty of the Village was its hospitality. A part of its produce was set apart for the discharge of this duty in the Village Rest-house, wherein travellers were lodged and fed. The watchman met the traveller, took charge of his weapons, and, after ascertaining his name, etc., took him to the Rest-house ; when his stay was over, the watchman conducted him to the Village boundary, gave him back his weapons, and saw him off the premises, as it were. The watchman needed to be careful, for he was responsible if goods were stolen, having to make good their value to the robbed. The

Āryans were a practical people ; they evidently said : " Why pay a watchman if we are to be robbed ? " And the principle was carried out, for if a man was living in a kingdom and was robbed, he had a right to claim from the royal treasury four times the value of the object of which he had been improperly deprived. The Village heart, however, was not hard even to the disreputable, for a basket of food was hung up at night on a convenient tree, lest any objectionable person should be hungry, yet shun the light.

I may mention here that when villages extended and met, becoming towns, and when towns and villages were grouped into Republics under Councils, or into Kingdoms and Empires, the Pañchāyat idea still persisted, and the village officers reappeared with larger duties. In Madras, the Presidency capital, the names of its districts still bear the names of the old villages by the grouping of which they were formed, the termination of their names as districts being the old words for "village". The ancient office of a member for an old Pañchāyat reappears as that of a modern councillor for a ward in the municipality. Even now in a large field or open space, little huts spring up, and presently a board appears with the name of a street ; or a fishing village links itself with a weaving village, and presently the old "cheris" above spoken of reappear.

Even great Empires reproduce Village Pañchayats, and Kautilya tells us how the Imperial Council of Chandragupta Maurya, in the fourth century B.C., was made up of six Pañchāyats, each one governing a Department of the State.

Kautilya, in describing the duties of the village accountant, shows us how his duties extended as villages were grouped together. He has to set up:

"Boundaries to villages, by numbering plots of land as cultivated, uncultivated, plains, wet lands, gardens, vegetable gardens, fences, forests, altars, temples of Devas, irrigation works, cremation grounds, feeding-houses, places where water is freely supplied to travellers, places of pilgrimage, pasture-grounds and roads, and thereby fixing the boundaries of various villages, of fields, of forests and of roads; he shall register gifts, sales, charities, and remission of taxes regarding fields.

"Also having numbered the houses as tax-paying or non-tax-paying, he shall not only register the total number of the inhabitants of all the four castes in each village, but also keep an account of the exact number of the cultivators, cow-herds, merchants, artisans, labourers, slaves, and biped and quadruped animals, fixing at the same time the amount of gold, free labour, toll and fines that can be collected from it (each house).

"He shall also keep an account of the number of young and old men that reside in each house, their history, occupation, income and expenditure."

The duties of an accountant in the fourth century B.C. were evidently no sinecure.

As slaves are mentioned in this extract, and as Megasthenes remarked that there were no slaves (in the part of India he knew), it may be well to say a word on this subject.

Megasthenes says: " None of the Indians employ slaves. . . . All Indians are free and not one of them is a slave. . . . The Indians do not even use aliens as slaves, and much less a countryman of their own." (Fragment XXVII.) Dr. Banerjea, however, points out that a mild form of slavery did exist, and says that the Dāsas, or servants, were originally Dāsyus, non-Āryans captured in war; their children remained slaves, and criminals were sometimes condemned to slavery as a punishment. They could, however, purchase their freedom, they could not be sold, and ill-treatment was severely punished. They were part of the family, and to free them was considered meritorious. Dr. Banerjea also states that the institution died out, and it may have disappeared generally when Megasthenes wrote. Kautilya gives the law concerning slaves, and it was certainly a very mild form of slavery. Among the Āryans, if a minor were sold or mortgaged by kinsmen, these latter were fined and the purchasers and abettors were punished. " Never," he writes, " shall an Ārya be subjected to slavery." If his life were mortgaged " to tide over family troubles," his kinsmen must redeem him as soon as possible. Non-Āryan slaves were not only protected from ill-usage generally, but women were specially guarded: the violation of a woman slave set her free, and if a child were born it also was free. (See Book III, pp. 230-233.)

A mark of the general high character of the people was the fact that contracts were verbal, not written and money and articles of value were deposited for safe keeping without receipts being given.

No surprise need be felt about this long-continued and well-organized Village System, since English observers have remarked on the fact that Local Self-Government is a characteristic of the East. Kingdoms change their boundaries; empires last for a comparatively brief time, if we except the Empire of the Pāndavas, of whom Prithvirāj was the last royal descendant. Consider the following clearly-expressed opinions of thoughtful Englishmen:

Sir John Lawrence said as long ago as 1864:

"The people of India are quite capable of administering their own affairs and the municipal feeling is deeply rooted in them.

"The village communities, each of which is a little republic, are the most abiding of Indian institutions. Holding the position we do in India, every view of duty and policy should induce us to leave as much as possible of the business of the country to be done by the people."

Sir Bartle Frere, in 1871, wrote:

"Anyone who has watched the working of Indian society will see that its genius is one to represent, not merely by election under Reform Acts, but represent generally by provisions, every class of the community, and when there is any difficulty respecting any matter to be laid before Government, it should be discussed among themselves. When there is any fellow-citizen to be rewarded or punished, there is always a caste meeting, and this is an expression, it seems to me, of the genius of the people, as it was of the old Saxons, to gather together in assemblies of different types to vote by tribes or hundreds."

As Mr. Chisholm Anstey said:

"We are apt to forget in this country, when we talk of preparing people in the East by education, and all that sort of thing, for Municipal Government and Parliamentary Government (if I may use such a term), that the East, is the parent of Municipalities. Local Self-Government, in the widest acceptation of the term, is as old as the East itself. No matter what may be the religion of the people who inhabit what we call the East, there is not a portion of the country from west to east, from north to south, which is not swarming with municipalities, and not only so, but like to our municipalities of old, they are all bound together as in a species of net-work, so that you have ready-made to your hand the frame-work of a great system of representation."

Such quotations might be largely multiplied. Wherever the masses are left to themselves to manage their own associations, they quickly establish a Pañchāyat and readily obey its directions; it is their traditional form of government, and they instinctively yield it obedience, while looking with suspicion and distrust on other forms of government.

The argument that Democracy is foreign to India

cannot be alleged by any well-informed person. Maine and other historians recognized the fact that Democratic Institutions are essentially Āryan, and spread from India to Europe with the immigration of Āryan peoples; Pañchāyats, the "village republics," have been the most stable institution of India, and only vanished during the last century under the pressure of the East India Company's domination. They still exist within the castes, each caste forming within itself a thorough democracy, in which the same man may have as relations a prince and peasant. Social rank does not depend so much on wealth and titles as on learning and occupation. India is democratic in spirit, and in institutions left to her from the past and under her control in the present.

B.—Its Present

The present condition of the Indian Village is a heart-breaking contrast to its Past, and when we consider the huge number of villages in India, we realise that if India, as a Nation, is not to pass away, she must be rescued from that fate by restoring the villages to their former prosperity. The total population of India in 1921 was 316,017,751; out of these only 32,418,776 lived in towns, and 283,598,975 lived in "rural territory," that is in places with a population of less than 5,000 persons. There are only 35 towns with populations of 100,000 and over; only 54 with populations between 50,000 and 100,000.

Then we have 199 towns with populations between 20,000 and 50,000; 450 with populations between 10,000 and 20,000; 885 with populations between 5,000 and 10,000; and 690 with populations under 5,000. There are only two towns, Calcutta and Bombay, with populations of over one million. I give these details, so that readers may realise the immensity ot the village problem in India: even if we subtract the population of the Indian States, it leaves in "British" India no less than 247,003,293 human beings.

The total area of India is 1,773,165 square miles; of this the Indian States occupy 675,267 square miles, leaving 1,097,898 for the Provinces under British Rule. (These figures do not include Burma and Ceylon, which are usually included when the figures are taken for "the Indian Empire".) Over these 1,097,898 square miles are scattered, according to the *Statistical Abstract* published by Government in 1923, 497,911 villages.

With a population—		Villages
Under 500 persons there are	..	364,138
Of 500-1,000 persons there are	..	82,265
Of 1,000-2,000 persons there are	..	38,313
Of 2,000-5,000 persons there are	..	13,195
Total number	..	497,911

(In the Indian States there are 186,849 villages, and in speaking of the number these are often added in, and the joint number is put roughly at 700,000.) It will be noticed that there are only 133,773 villages the population of which is over 500, so that in the large majority the areas are of manageable size.

Let us consider how these peoples' lives were affected by the destruction of their Village System.

Four great changes were made by this destruction:

1. Peasant proprietors were substituted for the holding of land by the Village.

2. Officials responsible to the Government were substituted for officers elected by the villagers from among themselves.

3. Factory-made goods and foreign goods replaced the products of village industries, and destroyed the export trade which brought wealth.

4. A changed method of Government taxation was created, money of a fixed amount instead of a fixed proportion of the crop; and new incomprehensible laws were made by an alien Rule ignorant of immemorial usages. It is well to remember these four, though in dealing with them they cannot be separated.

Peasant proprietors were created in the South of India by the "raiyatwari" system in 1816 by Sir Thomas Monro. Mr. J. Rangachari gives the following account of its beginnings:

"The villages and the village community were broken up. Those till then its servants were turned into its masters and instruments of oppression. . . . We have seen that the village acted as a body. The Village Assembly did everything on behalf of the village. But on the introduction of the Raiyatwari settlement, the revenue official dealt with the individual raiyat, setting aside the Village community. Every raiyat was granted a patta (document) for the land he cultivated, defining his rent, etc., and he was informed that he was to continue to cultivate this land of which he was put in possession so long as he paid the land-tax thereon, and in no case was it ever left to the raiyats to change their lands either annually or practically. Moreover the revenue officials exercised the right of transferring a land to any raiyat, if the original holder was unwilling or unable to pay the revenue fixed on it. . . . In some districts the conversion was effected by the inhabitants assembling together and drawing lots in the usual manner, but under condition that they should keep permanently the land which fell to them, and for which they afterwards applied to the Collector for patta."

The land is re-assessed at intervals, and numerous instances occur where the peasant is forced to borrow to pay the increased assessment.

The huge indebtedness of the peasant cultivator is the despair of all who try to help him. Sir Dinshah Wacha has pointed out that this load of debt is constantly increasing. Land revenue also increased by 80,000,000 rupees between 1882 and 1907. The salt tax in the budget of two years ago was raised by

9,000,000 rupees, though a necessary of life. Let Gopāla Krishna Gokhalé once more speak:

> "Forty millions of people, according to one great Anglo-Indian authority—Sir William Hunter—pass through life with only one meal a day. According to another authority—Sir Charles Elliot—seventy millions of people in India do not know what it is to have their hunger fully satisfied even once in the whole course of the year. The poverty of the people of India, thus considered by itself, is truly appalling. And if this is the state of affairs after a hundred years of your rule, you cannot claim that your principal aim in India has been the promotion of the interests of the Indian people."

Land revenue rises almost every year: in 1910 it was 30.1 crores of rupees (a crore is 10,000,000). In the succeeding years it was, in crores: 33, 34, 34½, 34⅓, 35¾, 35¾, 35, 34, 36¾, 34¾. Taking the same decade for the total net revenue, we find that it begins with £74,600,000 sterling and rises to £144½.

The increasing indebtedness of the peasants is readily understood when we learn from a Government official, Mr. Alexander, Collector of Etawah, that "in ordinary years," the cultivators live for four months each year on advances from the money-lenders, who always charge a high rate of interest, and recover the loan, more often only a part of it, when the borrowers reap their crops. An official report reveals an even worse state of things:

"Small holdings are very common, and holders of land cannot be regarded as being above the condition of labourers. The yield that is obtained from the lands will probably maintain them for a period of six months, while in the remaining part of the year they are entirely left to the mercy of the sowcar (money-lender)."

Another way of increasing the indebtedness in the Madras Presidency is given by Mr. A. Ranganathan, a member of the Madras Legislative Council. He writes in a paper on "The Indian Village as it is":

"The cultivator finds it difficult in any case to pay this high land-tax. But the Government makes it far worse by demanding the revenue due to them before he has time to gather his crops in. If the land-tax due by a cultivator is not paid on demand to the agents of the Government, the defaulter's property which may be the utensils in his house, or his milch cow, or the crops on the land or the land itself, may be proceeded against and the arrears realized by the sale thereof. Naturally, the raiyat submits himself to any hardship rather than have his property publicly attached for land revenue, and suffer in the estimation of the whole village. My work brings me into close contact with people in villages, and I can confidently assert that there are very few owners of land who are able to pay the Government dues, without soliciting outside help. They have to pay their taxes oftentimes while their crops are still in the fields, instead of waiting until they are harvested and the farmer can sell at a good price. So they are compelled to go to the money-lenders and borrow money at high rates of interest or on equally unfair terms. Very often they mortgage their crops in advance and undertake to sell these at some rate which is far lower than the prevailing market price, because of this short-sighted policy of the Government of insisting upon payment of the taxes in full before the raiyat can choose his time, and sell his crop at rates most favourable to himself. This borrowing so very often means that he has to go from year's end to year's end without the necessary sustenance in order to repay, or to carry on until at some later stage he again borrows money, and again at high rates of interest. If, on the other hand, the Government allowed the landholders sufficient time to collect all their produce, before they are asked to pay the dues of the Government, they would obtain fair prices for their produce and be in a position to sell on favourable terms, just so much of their produce as may be necessary and clear the Government dues."

Some time ago I studied the records made by Government officials on the condition of the small agriculturalists in the United Provinces ; Mr. Alexander's above statement is drawn from these. The Collector of Etah gives the case of a man with a large holding of 17 acres, whose deficiency on the land, with bare food and clothing, was Rs.138.9 in the year of enquiry. Another with seven acres, paid a rent of Rs.40 ; food Rs.50 ; clothing Rs.7 ; furniture Rs.2; marriage and funeral expenses Rs.2; deficit was Rs.22. Another had 5½ acres, a plough and a pair of oxen; he made a profit of Rs.45.14 in the year, on which he, and a family of four persons "lived". A fourth had 9 acres; rent Rs.68.15; sold his crops for Rs.70.4; made Rs.15 by outside labour, and sold milk from two cows for Rs.18. There are many more of these family budgets.

Professor Ganguli lectured last year on "The Indian Rural Problem" (published in the *Journal of the East Indian Association*; the date of the lecture, May 18th). He analysed the problem into five factors: (1) The minute sub-division of the land; (2) the necessity of borrowing from a money-lender "for the bare necessities of a primitive agricultural practice"; (3) the need of better marketing facilities; (4) the exhaustion of the soil; (5) the physical condition of the peasant. (1) is the result of peasant proprietorship instead of communal; (2) is because the peasant cannot raise enough on his little holding to support himself and his family, to say nothing of the land-tax and the high rate of interest on his borrowings; on (3) the professor points out, among other things, that "generally speaking, the greater portion of the prospective harvest is held in mortgage to the village trader". The professor gives the differences in prices of three important crops, between the mortgaged and the free crops. For the mortgaged crop of Jute the price of sale is from Rs.5.8 to Rs.6. For the free, Rs.8.10 to Rs.9. For Linseed, Rs.1.8 to Rs.1.12, compared with Rs.2.8 to Rs.2.13. For Grain, Rs.4.8 to Rs.5, compared with

Rs.6.12 to Rs.7. The exhaustion of the soil (4) is due to the extreme poverty of the peasant; he cannot get manure; the professor gives the annual average production of wheat in bushels per acre, in twelve countries: Belgium comes at the top with 37; India at the bottom with 12. As to (5) "the chief asset must be the output of physical energy of which the worker is capable. As the physical fitness cannot be easily assessed 'the expectation of life' at any specified age, may be taken as an indication of physical well-being." Five countries are given.

In Denmark a man of 20 may expect to live to 66.3; in England to 63.01; in Italy to 63.77; in Japan to 60.35. In India there is a sudden drop; a man of 20 can, on an average, only expect to live to 47.46. A man of 40 in Denmark may expect to live, on an average, to 69.7; in England to 63.96; in Italy to 68.23; in Japan to 66.03; but in India only to 58.02.

The average life-period of a man in India was given by Mr. Gokalé at 23.5; this was and is due to the enormous death-rate of infants during the first year of mortal life. This dangerous period is over in the lowest age given by Professor Ganguli. The shortening of life is chiefly due to semi-starvation. His figures of the shortage of food are appalling. The half of the peasants who used to be always hungry is now two-thirds. In his own words:

"One cannot challenge the conclusions of Professor Dayashankar Dubey that '64.6 per cent. of the population lives always on insufficient food, getting only about 73 per cent. of the minimum requirement for maintaining efficiency. In other words it clearly shows that two-thirds of the population always get only three-quarters of the amount of food-grains they should have.' But this state of semi-starvation is chiefly the result of persistent soil-erosion and soil-exhaustion, which have brought the greater part of the cultivated land to its fertility level, and if this is allowed to continue, the day of reckoning is not far."

In 1915, in the Indian National Congress, I pointed to the fact that the greatest danger threatening India was a "revolution of hunger". That danger is now nearer. In the eighteenth century Phillimore said of India that "the droppings of her soil fed distant regions". Two thousand years before, Megasthenes spoke of the "abundant means of existence" of the cultivators. The Government knows well enough the ghastly suffering, for one of its own Reports says:

"Occasional famine is only the pronounced expression of continuous scarcity, or, in other words, the complete failure of crops in certain parts of India, which are so severe as to attract public notice, are but as the deep and long-cast shadows of depression in the agricultural out-turn which occur almost every year; that the problem in fact of saving a portion of the population from misery and semi-starvation over vast areas of India is an annually recurring one. . . . The ancient rulers resorted from time immemorial to the expedient of storing water in the monsoon for utilisation during the subsequent dry weather."

Quite so. Then why have not the British Rulers followed the immemorial custom ? Why has it been left in Madras Presidency until, after the Reforms of 1919, an Indian has come into power, and, by following the example of his ancestors, the Hon. Sir C. P. Ramaswami Aiyar has succeeded in passing a Bill which, by irrigating 300,000 acres of land, will put an end to the " recurring " famines in that district ? He will deal with another recurring famine district in a few months.

It is worth remembering that, when Indians ruled Indians, Megasthenes remarked that " famine never visited India, and that there has never been a great scarcity in the supply of nourishing food."

I venture to repeat a summary made by myself of the villagers' grievances under British Rule.

The Forest Laws, made by Legislators inappreciative of village difficulties, press hardly on them, and only in a small number of places have Forest Pañchāyats been established. In the few cases in which the experiment has been made the results have been good, in some cases marvellously good. The paucity of grazing grounds for their cattle, the lack of green manure to feed their impoverished lands, the absence of fencing round forests, so that the cattle, straying when feeding, are impounded and have to be redeemed, the fines and other punishments for offences ill-understood, the want of wood for fuel, for tools, for repairs, the uncertain distribution of the available water, all these troubles are discussed in villages and in local conferences. The Arms Act oppresses them by leaving them defenceless against wild beasts and wild men. The union between Judicial and Executive functions makes justice often inaccessible and always costly both in money and in time.

On this last point let us listen to Mr. Ranganathan :

"The people suffer also in regard to the administration of Justice. When referring to the Village Headmen I stated that they, as a rule, combined in themselves the offices of Magistrates and of Civil Judge. But it is one thing to give them the power to try cases and another to create sufficient trust in their integrity and impartiality among the people so that they may freely utilise the services of the Headman to dispose of their petty Civil and Criminal cases. Enough has been said to show how the short-sighted changes introduced by the British brought about diversities of interests and lack of good-will between the villagers and their local officers, with the consequence that the gulf between them has been widening so far that the common folk have come to regard the village officials as irresponsible representatives of an unsympathetic bureaucracy and think it futile to expect fair play and justice at their hands. So people requiring judicial redress now go long distances to file their cases before the regular tribunals and are obliged to be constantly away from their villages to be present during the enquiry of their cases. This means not only great dislocation of work at home and loss of income for the days they are absent from the village, but, in addition, considerable expense and inconvenience to all concerned in the cases.

"It is comparatively in a few classes of cases that Courts in India are permitted the help of jurors or assessors. The trying Magistrate or Judge has generally no local knowledge of the conditions or habits of the people who appear before him. As the enquiry takes place as a rule far from the place of offence of the cause of action, there is not available, at the place of enquiry, that public opinion which, being acquainted with the facts of the case, can immediately and effectively check any tendencies towards exaggeration or prevarication on the part of parties or witnesses to a case. In the old days, the old village Pañchāyat would deal with the civil and criminal cases of comparatively less serious character, and dispose of them in their own village. Instead of that they now have to go long distances in order to have their cases heard. You will understand the inconvenience that is caused to the people, especially when I tell you that in Madras, there is one Criminal Court for every 55 villages or 150 square miles. And one Civil Court for every 212 villages or 575 square miles. Think of all the trouble the people are now put to to obtain justice. Justice, if it is to be worth anything at all, should be cheap and prompt, instead of which it is extremely costly and doubtful whether it is obtainable at all. The truth can be known only in the villages and not by people living far away, who have no knowledge of the habits or veracity of the people they are dealing with. In my own experience, I have had to deal with such cases, when acting as a Government Officer. On one occasion, I had a man come to me with a complaint. I asked him to state his case, and in the end he alleged that his house had been broken into and that some jewels and other things had been stolen. I felt there was something wrong, and still I did not know how I could, on the mere statement of the man, come to the conclusion that his story was not true. Some time after, without telling anybody, I went to the man's village, and, in the presence of the villagers there, asked him what he had to say, and I was surprised when the man bluntly said that his complaint was not true. Do you think that this man was suddenly filled with remorse and wanted to tell the truth ? No. But he knew it was no use, and would be unwise to give his testimony in the village, where I had the means of checking myself his statement, whereas I had it not before. He knew he would be contradicted by the people there if he made any untrue statements. I was thus able to give justice to the other man, better than if I had dealt with the case a long way off. That is one of the defects of the present method of administering justice."

The self-contained character of the Indian village, spoken of by Sir Charles Metcalfe (see Introduction), has largely disappeared at the present time, as the result of the destruction of the self-ruled village, with its Pañchāyat, elected annually, its artisans and craftsmen, its village servants and the interdependence of all its inhabitants. Mr. A. Ranganathan writes:

"In the old days the village had its carpenter, blacksmith and people of similar avocations. Their duty was to attend to the preparation and repair of the implements of the villagers, to manufacture all the vessels they required, and things of that sort. These people also had some lands given them free of tenure or on favourable terms, and, like the other village officials, were receiving some emoluments from the people of the village. The Government have taken over the control of these service lands, with the result that these artisans grew very reluctant to discharge their duties to the people, and the people, on the other side, do not feel compelled to give them their share, as they did in the old days, to give them their emoluments which were their due, so that a number of these villages now have no artisans of their own, and the cultivators have to go to neighboring villages to get their tools made and their implements repaired. And the number of villages in this position is increasing, as I can safely testify from my own knowledge. The result is that an unfortunate villager, who may have a plough needing repair, has to take it to a far-off village to get it attended to, instead of, as hitherto, getting it attended to in his own village."

Villagers have made similar complaints to myself; I have written elsewhere, and poor men have told me, of the difficulties they have to meet; it was easy to cultivate plots for the carpenter, the ironsmith, the weaver; in return the tools and the implements were kept in good order, cloths were supplied, so that both sides profited and neither side suffered. A purely agricultural village cannot be self-contained, prosperous or contented. Much is heard in these days about Hindu-Musalmān troubles, but foreigners do not probably realize that these scarcely ever occur in the villages; they are almost entirely confined to the towns. The reason is a very simple one. Village parents tend to bring up their children to pursue their own type of gaining a livelihood. (A very intelligent son will be sent to a town school, will go on to the University, and become a doctor, a lawyer, an engineer. The rest of the family will follow the occupation of their parents.) Hinḍus and Musalmāns in the same village tend to follow separate occupations, and thus become interdependent, and cannot afford, are not inclined, to quarrel seriously, much less to break out into riots. When villagers quarrel, they go to law as a rule; they do not fight.

The results of the insufficient food, continuing year after year, on the vitality of the peasants are definitely shown by their slight resistance to epidemics, and to all forms of disease. In the influenza epidemic whole villages were depopulated, and the death-rate was doubled in India as a whole. The infantile mortality is always shocking. The death-rate of a decade per mille of boys under a year, in the last *Statistical Abstract*, omitting 1918, the influenza year, was: 214, 216, 192, 218, 208, 209, 211, 228, 201. The death-rate of girls was 196, 198, 196, 204, 195, 194, 198, 220, 188. There are two main causes—the low vitality of the peasants, always underfed, and, in the large villages, the bad sanitary conditions with lack of doctors and dispensaries. Despite all pleading the Governments recognize only the western medical system, though the masses of the people flock always, if they get the chance, to a doctor practising the ancient systems. The first Medical College for the ancient systems was founded in Madras by the efforts of an Indian Minister three years ago, against the furious opposition of the foreign medical men. Yet their numbers are ridiculously small compared with the vast Indian population. Among the workers in factories the death-rate among babies throws the above figures into the shade. H.E. Lady Wilson, the wife of the Governor of Bombay, speaking on infant mortality in Bombay, placed it at 622 per mille, but the year was not given. Other years were mentioned by her when the mortality was 400 and 300. It is not surprising that Professor Ganguli, realising that two-thirds of the Indian population get, year after year, only three-quarters of the food they need for decent health, says that "it is clear that the time has come for decisive action". India is literally dying slowly from semi-starvation, an agonising prolonged death. It began in the second half of the eighteenth century, when we read of the awful famine of 1770, of which the *Imperial Gazetteer* says:

"The Hooghly every day rolled down thousands of corpses close to the porticoes and gardens of the English conquerors. The very streets of Calcutta were blocked up by the dying and the dead. . . . (It was) officially reported to have swept away two-thirds of the inhabitants." (*Loc. cit.*, ii 480.)

Between 1770 and 1900—130 years—there were twenty-two serious famines, as well as the recurring minor ones and the continual semi-starvation. I saw the famines of 1896 and 1899, and wrote of "the night-mare railway stations, into which living skeletons forced their way, holding out skinny hands and crying out in agony to the passengers for food."

We have seen the prosperity of Indian villages in the Past—their normal state through millennia. We have seen the Government Report from which a quotation is given above, stating that "famine is only the pronounced expression *of continuous scarcity*" (italics mine). British Rule has wrought this change in a century and three-quarters. If it be true that an ancient Indian Sage warned a young King to beware of the sorrows of the weak, "for the tears of the weak undermine the throne of Kings," surely it is well for Britain as well as for India that some should strive to win for this ancient land the Freedom which alone can save her from perishing. Only Self-Rule can rescue her. And there is hope when, as I wrote last year, an Indian Executive Councillor "has faced the horror of the annual recurrence of famine, and is grappling with it with every prospect of success, at least in the Madras Presidency; and he meets it in the old Indian way—by irrigation, turning desert into fertile soil. From this one striking illustration, we may judge something of the possibilities which open before us, when India ceases to be a tributary

State, drained of men and money for the advantage of the British Empire, her Nationals treated with contumely all over that Empire, except in Britain itself, and even in her own land allowed only 'a share' in the Government, a share which can at times be suspended by the unfair use of 'emergency powers'." Other Indians in other Provinces will surely follow in the steps of C. P. Ramaswami Aiyar, when India comes to her own, and turns herself to the recovery of what she was in her splendid Past.

C.—The Remedy

The only remedy for the present condition of Indian villages is legislation in the Imperial Parliament of Great Britain. Not long ago Lord Birkenhead, His Majesty's Secretary of State for India, announced that the present Government would consider any measure proposed by Indian leaders. Such a Bill—the Commonwealth of India Bill—has been officially adopted after full consideration by His Majesty's Opposition in Parliament, led by the late Prime Minister, the Rt. Hon. Ramsay MacDonald, P.C., after its first reading in the House of Commons last December (1925), and its being ordered to be printed. This Bill is the fruit of the active agitation for Home Rule, following the resolution in the Indian National Congress of 1914, asking that India might be placed on an equality with the Self-Governing Dominions; the history of this agitation will be found in chapters IV. and V. on "The Awakening of India" and "Home Rule for India". This Bill was drafted by the Convention of 1924-5 after three years of work, including two Conferences in February, 1923 and 1924, which outlined the scheme, organised a propaganda for it, and finally merged itself into a Convention which met in April, 1924. The story will be found in chapter V. "Home Rule for India". Suffice it to say here that these bodies were composed of 231 members of the Legislative Central and Provincial (elected since the Reform Act of 1919), 19 elected representatives of the National Home Rule League, and 26 others, some elected and some prominent Indian leaders, like Sir Tej Bahadur Sapru, K.C.S.I., late Law Member of the Governor-General's Council, who was elected President of the Conferences and Convention, and the Rt. Hon. V. S. Srinivasa Sastri, P.C., elected Vice-President. It would be difficult to find a more representative body.

To my mind the most vital feature of this Bill is not so much that which gives India Dominion status, "a Free State in a Federation of Free States owing allegiance to His Imperial Majesty the King Emperor," as stated in the Preamble, but the revival of the ancient type of Local Self-Government, in the Villages, the group of Villages (Taluka) and the grouped Talukas (District).

This is built up from the bottom in the old way, from the Village.

The principles are laid down which each Provincial Council shall apply in its own Province; these sub-Provincial authorities "shall exercise the rights of

Self-Government," the Village having its Pañchāyat, the Taluka its Sabhā, the rural District its Samiti, the Urban its Municipality. All may appoint Committees with delegated power and duties.

All electors must have reached the age of 21 and upwards.

The suffrage is graded: Every resident villager has a vote for the Pañchāyat. For the Taluka Sabhā, the elector must be resident and have *one* of the following qualifications:

1. All members or ex-members of village pañchāyats.

2. All literates in a language of the Taluka, or persons trained in a village workshop, or skilled in some craft.

3. All who have a monthly income or allowance of Rs.10 and above.

4. All owners and occupiers of land with Rs.10 per annum or more as land-tax.

5. All owning or occupying a house, or a part of it, of the annual rental value of Rs.6.

For the District (there are 26 in Madras Presidency, which has over 40 millions of inhabitants) the elector must be a resident and have *one* of the following qualifications:

1. All members or ex-members of Taluka Sabhās or Ward Pañchāyats.

2. All with primary, or equivalent technical, education.

3. All who have a monthly income or allowance of Rs.15 and above.

4. All owners or occupiers of land with Rs.20 per annum or more as land-tax.

5. All owning or occupying a house, or a part of it, of the annual rental of Rs.18 or more.

(The rupee varies in value as regards English money, from 1*s*. 4*d*. to 1*s*. 6*d*.)

It will be noticed that the qualifications for electors in larger areas than the village are: (1) a little knowledge of administration and having won the confidence of his fellows; (2) or an amount of education enabling him to know what is going on in the area; or manual ability making him useful; (3) or some wage or pension, 13*s*. 8*d*. in the one case, £1 in the other; (4) or paying a small rent to the State for the use of its land; (5) or a very low rent.

Qualifications for members of these bodies are also laid down; it must be remembered that our Āryan forefathers were very much more practical than their descendants in Europe, after they were demoralised by feudalism, as was shown, *inter alia*, by their village watchman being compelled, if there was a theft in the village, either to recover the article or pay its value unless he could trace it out of the village, the King being liable to pay from his treasury four times the value of the stolen article; why pay for protection and not obtain it? Hence they required knowledge or capacity in those they elected to administer areas not under the eyes of the persons they elected to discharge responsible duties. All the villagers knew their village affairs and each other. So all villagers could be electors and members. But what did the villager know of a great group of villages, a hundred or a thousand, the needs of their people, or the capacities of those elected to look after them ?

So members of a Taluka Sabhā or a District Samiti must not be less than 25 years of age. In the former he must have had primary education, or have been an ex-member of a Village Pañchāyat for a full term. In the latter, he must have had secondary (middle school) education, or be an ex-member of a Taluka or Ward Sabhā for a full term.

It will be noted that with a school once more in every village, free and compulsory, all the boys and girls when they are 21 will have a vote for the Sabhā and the Samiti ; and this will be automatic ; there will be no need for more Suffrage Bills.

Let us consider now the respective powers and duties of these three bodies. These are classified under three heads, and others could, of course, be added, if found necessary. But it will be seen how serious and responsible will be the work of these sub-Provincial authorities :

The Powers of the Village Panchayat

" (*a*) *Education and Recreation.*—Primary schools, village workshops, libraries, parks, gymnasia, recreation grounds, etc.

" (*b*) *Protection.*—Control over erection of buildings, sanitation and conservancy, prevention of public nuisances, fairs and festivals, medical help and village dispensary, control over offensive and dangerous trades, village cattle pounds, registration of births and deaths, civil and criminal jurisdiction in simple cases exercised by a court of summary jurisdiction, village police, local militia, if any.

" (*c*) *Economic and Industrial Ministration.*—Co-operative stores and banks, wells, tanks and canals, cottage industries, village irrigation, village fairs, cattle stands, village forests and grazing grounds, roads and bridges, certain powers of local taxation and other works of public utility handed over by the Taluka Sabhā."

Powers of the Taluka Sabha

" (*a*) *Education and Recreation.*—Lower secondary or middle school education, technical schools, model farms.

" (*b*) *Protection.*—Control over markets, fairs, etc., hospitals and dispensaries, civil criminal jurisdiction in simple cases or in appeals from village cases exercised by a specially appointed bench of magistrates, decision of disputes between villages, control in cases of epidemics, co-ordination of village police, Taluka police or reserve force.

" (*c*) *Economic and Industrial Ministration.*—Stock of agricultural machinery for hire, stud animals, supplies of seeds suitable for different soils in the Taluka, main roads between villages, small irrigation channel, promotion of village industries, other works of public utility handed over to the Taluka Board by the District Samiti, central co-operative stores and banks for helping village stores and banks."

POWERS OF THE DISTRICT SAMITI (RURAL) OR MUNICIPALITY (URBAN).

" (*a*) *Education and Recreation.*—Higher secondary or high school and college education. Technical college, a technical institute studying soils, manures, crops.

" (*b*) *Protection.*—Co-ordination of Taluka police, district police or special reserve, larger hospitals and dispensaries, inspection of foodstuffs, epidemic disease, public health, settlement of disputes between Taluka boards, civil and criminal jurisdiction within fixed limits, and deciding sanctioned appeals from Taluka benches by a specially appointed bench of magistrates.

" (*c*) *Economic and Industrial Ministration.*—Co-ordinating local stores and banks and other village enterprises of an industrial or commercial nature and model farms, supply of information needed by cultivators, craftsmen and others, stores of seeds for supplying Taluka and model farms, forests, district roads, district waterways and railways, district bridges, levying cess and raising loans within prescribed limits, allocating provincial subsidies among Taluka Boards if necessary.

" Provided that District Samitis (Rural) or Municipalities (Urban) are empowered as far as possible to own all public means of transport, lighting, water-supply, markets within their area and to utilise the profit for decreasing taxation."

When this Bill becomes law, the gradual up-building of India will begin. The chief danger will arise from the habit of centralisation, caught by the Intelligentsia from their English Education, and in most cases of official habits forced upon them by English official superiors. They are all so accustomed to delegate powers from above, that they cannot believe in the exercise of powers on the initiative of the person acting.

Mr. W. R. Gourlay, I.C.S., Director of Agriculture and Co-operative Credit Societies, Bengal, speaks from experience of village life :

"The majority of cultivators within their own villages have a character for honest dealing among their neighbors, and it is this character for honesty which is the basis of all co-operative credit.

"The villagers pledge their character as security for their loans." (*Madras Bulletin*, September, 1909.)

The same fact is often noted by those who form small Co-operative Credit Societies among the very poor.

But Lord Ronaldshay and the Earl of Lytton, successively Governors of Bengal, give their own testimony to what they have seen of the working of the Bengal Union Boards Act, and their testimony is beyond dispute. (A Union Board is a Board superintending several villages, practically a Taluka Board.)

I will make no apology for a long quotation, because of its high authority. It is taken from Lord Ronaldshay's book, *India: A Bird's Eye View.* He remarks that the system "was suitable to Indian tradition," and makes some rather sharp remarks on the way the English insist on forcing their own institutions in countries they dominate, quoting Emerson's remark (noted above in the Introduction) that:

"'The Englishman sticks to his traditions and usages, and, so help him God, he will force his island bye-laws down the throat of great countries like India, China, Canada, Australia'" (p. 125).

He says:

"It must be admitted that, in deciding upon the type of local authority to be established in India, the authorities of the day went a long way towards justifying that somewhat caustic criticism" (p. 126).

After commenting on the result in India, he proceeds:

"The result was not altogether happy, and a people with a less robust belief in the excellence of their own institutions, might indeed have found cause for discouragement at the manner in which the useful if somewhat unambitious sphere of municipal administration at any rate, the great principle of 'Government by the people and for the people' was given application" (*ibid*). "Existing institutions are, to a considerable degree, alien from the spirit of the people" (p. 131).

Lord Ronaldshay deals with the Past of India, and the Guilds with their own laws which the King did not make:

"Such laws, according to the ancient law-books of the country, commanded recognition at the hands of the King (i.e. the central government), who was further charged with the duty of seeing that they were respected. That 'cultivators, traders, herdsmen, money-lenders, and artisans have authority to lay down laws for their respective classes,' is asserted by Gautama some centuries B.C., and that 'the King must discipline and establish again on the path of duty all such as have erred from their own laws, whether families, castes, guilds, associations, or people of certain districts,' is emphasized by Yajnavalkya. These bodies, therefore, were independent of the central government; they were not its offspring, nor were their functions the product of devolution, as in the case of such bodies as the borough and county councils of Great Britain. On the contrary, they were social organizations with authority which was not derived from, but which compelled the recognition of, the central government. Side by side with, or out of, these early guilds came into being village assemblies modelled on similar lines and possessing an equivalent status, which seem to have exercised judicial and municipal powers, and to have administered endowments for secular and religious purposes (pp. 132, 133). . . .

"I have devoted some space to a consideration of the system of administration in force in Ancient India because of the obvious bearing which it has upon the question which I have been discussing, namely, the unsuitability of the particular type of local self-government which we have instituted to the genius of the Indian people. It is, I think, a not unreasonable deduction from the knowledge which we now possess of the theory and practice of government in Ancient India that if, instead of creating municipal and district boards of the Western type, we had begun by re-creating the village organizations which were congenial to the people, local self-government would have made more satisfactory progress than has actually been the case. The steps which have been taken in various parts of India in recent years to establish village self-governing bodies have been handicapped by the prior existence of district and local boards. Instead of being the foundation of the whole edifice, they have had to be tacked on to the already existing institutions, and difficulty has, consequently, been experienced in fitting them into the general scheme (pp. 139, 140).

". . . It was not until 1919 that a special Act known as the Bengal Village Self-Government Act was passed with the object of placing union boards as far as possible upon a sound statutory basis, and of providing for the creation of village courts and benches.

This salutary return in the direction of the ancient indigenous system is breathing new life into local self-government. Let me conduct the reader to a Bengal village, the scene of the activities of a newly founded union board (p. 189).

"To such a village in the Dacca district I came not long after the passing of the Village Self-Government Act of 1919, to meet the members of the union board; and was conducted to a pandal erected in a small open space, the counterpart of the English village green. All round the pandal in perspiring groups stood the sparsely clad population of the village, interested spectators of what was going forward. In front of me in the centre of the pandal stood a table, on which were placed the books of the union board; and round me were seated the members of the board, bearded and reverend seigneurs, men who carried the confidence of their fellow-villagers. . . .

"A small tax known as the chaukidari tax for the upkeep of the village police is a compulsory levy; but under the Village Self-Government Act, a union board may impose additional taxation to enable it to undertake various works for the benefit of the villagers. I was shewn the accounts. The board, though of recent creation, had imposed additional taxation amounting to a quarter of the chaukidari tax. Did the villagers object? I asked. At first, yes; but it was explained that the board wanted the money for the construction of certain wells. Now above all things the villagers wanted wells, for a supply of good drinking water was a long-felt want. They would see what the board could do. The board, it seemed, did very well; and during the coming year the rate of taxation was to be doubled for further improvements. Presently I saw the wells, excellent circular shafts lined with brick, some feet in diameter, and with a neat coping round the top. The cost had been Rs. 300—£20—per well, and neither the district board nor any other agency, I was told, could construct such wells for less than double the sum; for the village had done the work itself; the chairman of the board had kept the accounts and done all the clerical work; a member of the board had supervised construction; the labor had come from the village itself. There had been, in fact, no middleman charges, and the village had got the full value of every rupee spent. The year before, twenty-five of the boards in the district had raised no revenue by taxation other than that of the chaukidari tax; this year all but fourteen of the one hundred and thirty union boards which had been established within the area had levied additional rates (144—146). . . .

"The trial of petty criminal cases and civil suits was a function of the guilds of ancient India, and the experimental establishment of village courts and benches under the Act of 1919 met with immediate success. In the year 1921, 652 criminal cases and 2,218 civil suits were instituted before fourteen such courts and benches, a single village court disposing of 260 civil suits and 66 criminal cases.

"It would seem, therefore, that the village is still the fundamental unit in the communal life of India; and it is worth noting in passing, as significant of the feelings of the village population, that at a recent conference of representatives of union boards in the Dacca district, a proposal was put forward for discussion for the abolition of district boards. More significant still, the proposal was carried (p. 148)."

Lord Lytton, the present Governor of Bengal, has given similar testimony, and he has stated that, on his return to England he will make the competency of these Union Boards an argument for giving the consent of Parliament to Home Rule.

Bengal has proved what Indians can do when they are given a chance and left to use it. The very name, the Village Self-Government Act of 1919, is in itself an encouragement. If the Union Boards had been called Taluka Sabhās it would have been still better, for each Union Board has a number of villages under it, as in our Commonwealth of India Bill.

In Madras Presidency a number of different Pañchāyats have been formed for different purposes; we have Village Pañchāyats, Village Forest Pañchāyats, Village Courts; each works well, even admirably, but there should be one Village Pañchāyat, with its Committees, as mentioned in Section (a), with its Committees, making a dignified body, and co-ordinating all village affairs, as in Dewan Bahadur's admirable Pañchāyat Act, fully discussed by the leading politicians of Madras in the "Madras Parliament" (a local Debating Society; see Chapter IV), followed in the Commonwealth of India Bill, now before the British House of Commons, read a first time, and ordered to be printed by it.

Bombay Presidency has also Village Pañchāyats

and District Boards; but the Village Pañchāyat has a limited suffrage, the District Board universal suffrage. Both in Madras and Bombay the old tradition is ignored.

I began by saying that for the establishment of Indian Local Government legislation is necessary. Voluntary effort might not succeed, but it must be tried, if we cannot obtain the old system by any other means.

One other fact that Lord Ronaldshay mentions is significant. He was asking what the villagers thought of the work of the Union Board, and he tells how an elderly man of good presence asked to speak. They had been discussing a tank; he said he was a pilot and had worked in local vessels all his life; his village needed a tank, and he laid before Lord Ronaldshay a good sum towards the making of it.

I once summarised the way of old India in a lecture on the Revival of the Pañchāyat, as follows:

"Villages were helped partly by communal enterprise and partly by benefactions such as this elderly man of to-day gave. It was in that way that the villages were made such satisfactory places to live in: they controlled their own taxation, they had labor, voluntary, unpaid, and all the village provided this by giving their work. You can see at once that amongst a people who live frugally, who are not in search of luxuries, but who live pleasantly, that a system of this sort, where you have small areas, where laborers are willing to labor, where those who can keep accounts are willing to keep accounts, with co-operation throughout the village, and where they see the way their own money is spent, instead of having to pay taxes which find their way into the hands of some superior officers and the villagers never know what has become of the money they have contributed, will be successful. I find it is true of the Indian, the poorer classes especially, that they are ever willing to give their work or money for anything which they can see, which results either in work for the village to which they belong, or advantage to the village as a whole. A good deal of the communal feeling has departed, but if we can see again that village land is appropriated to the village, if we can undo the work of the last century and let the people feel that the land on which they live belongs to themselves, that everything that is put into it will be a benefit to themselves, any work they do for it is a work which makes the whole village the better for it, I know from what I have seen that you will have many bands of self-respecting people who will take a deep interest in their village, and the fact that they are able to make it looked up to by less fortunate villages will encourage them. And it is this feeling of loyalty and duty to the Society in which they live, which is of the very essence of the Indian character, because there has always been the idea of obligation to the family, to the community. Utilising that feeling, which has come down through untold generations, using that to the uttermost, you will have again that enterprise and that wealth which was the heritage of India for thousands of years."

I began by saying that for the establishment of Indian Local Government legislation is necessary. The first voluntary effort made to accomplish it was, I believe, that made in Bihar in 1904 or 1905; a Pañchāyat Association was formed there, of which I had the honour of being President. It did not succeed, but started the idea. In 1916, at a Chittoor District Conference, over which I presided, I urged on the people the necessity of reviving the Village Pañchāyat, the Taluq Pañchāyat, the District Council, thus learning to administer successively larger areas as a preparation for the Self-Government of India.

We shall see under Education and under Industries, Chapters II and III, that the remedy for the present state of both begins in the Village.

II

EDUCATION

Its Past

ONE of the most splendid pages of the Past of India, if not *the* most splendid, since a Nation's conditions depend upon it, is that on which are written the records of its Education. These fall naturally into three marked periods, Ancient, Middle and Modern India, otherwise Vaidic, Buddhistic and Muslim. But these periods signify types of Education, and historically are not mutually exclusive; thus the Vaidic Period, exclusively Hindu, runs on with Hindu Universities through the Buddhist Period, in which we find Hindus and Buddhists studying side by side in the same Buddhist Universities; the Hindu also continues through the Muslim Period, but the latter is distinguished largely by the culture of its Imperial Courts, recalling those of Ancient and Early Middle India, and by its development of history. We find in all the three Periods a highly developed University Education for the classes in which deep learning was the object of life, and for those by which Government was carried on, the sons of Brāhmanas, of monarchs and nobles, and also of wealthy members of the great merchant community, the organizers of production and distribution: the sons of the two latter classes were trained in the

Universities in an understanding, not only of literature and science, but also of arts and crafts, so that on their return home they might intelligently examine and supervise their practical carrying out by artists, craftsmen and artisans, thus keeping up a high level of production in the villages, as well as setting a good example by attaching to their own courts or homes artists of special skill or of inborn genius, who produced their works at leisure, amply provided with the necessaries and comforts of life. We read how young princes, returning from some great University of their time, visited the village artificers to see that they were keeping up to the required level of excellence. It is also worthy of note that great religious Teachers of high rank, such as the Rishi Nārada, visited the courts of Kings, not merely to give instructions or guidance on high questions of policy, but also to enquire as to the matters which concerned the efficiency and prosperity of those employed in manual work, e.g. asking whether the artisans were properly supplied with the materials for their labor. Under these circumstances it was only natural that the Universities should train sons of the "twice-born castes" in the Shilpashāstras, previously mentioned, the Scriptures of Arts and Crafts.

Let us then first turn to the brilliant story of higher Education in India, the story of its Hindu, Buddhist and Muslim Universities and Colleges, not forgetting the Sangams of the South.

The highest Hindu intellectual training was based on the practice of yoga, and produced, as its fruit, those marvellous philosophical systems, the six Darshanas and the Brahma Sūtras, which are still the delight of scholars and the inspiration of Occultists and Mystics. The home of that training began in the recesses of the forests, wherein a great Sage would attract to his Āshrama (dwelling) numbers of pupils, whose faculties were there developed by the method of meditation, the working out of an abstruse problem, set by the teacher in a brief form, by intense and prolonged concentration upon it, aided by a simple and well-balanced and moderately ascetic life. This method of instruction explains two specialties of the Forest Āshrama: one was the huge numbers of pupils studying under a single Sage; a Sage was termed a Kulapati, lord of a family, when he fed and taught—he did not need to lodge—10,000 pupils. Later, we note that in some, at least, of the great Universities, the number of students under one teacher was limited to 500. The second was the occasionally great length of the student's life; men would remain, studying and meditating, till their hair had turned grey. And this was not confined to Forest Universities, for Professor Cowell—visiting the ancient University of Nadiyā—in Bengal, founded in the eleventh century, A.D.—writes in 1867:

"I could not help looking at these unpretending lecture halls with a deep interest, as I thought of the pandits lecturing there to generation after generation of eager inquisitive minds. Seated on the floor with his 'corona' of listening pupils round him, the teacher expatiates on those refinements of infinitesimal logic, which make a European's brain dizzy to think of, but whose labyrinth a trained Nadiya student will tread with unfaltering precision. I noticed during my visit middle-aged and even grey-haired men among the students."

Dr. Rabindranath Tagore has given us, in his *Tapovana*, a profoundly sympathetic sketch of this early stage of Indian learning :

" A most wonderful thing that we notice in Ancient India is, that here the forest not the town, is the fountain-head of all its civilization.

" Wherever, in India, its earliest and most wonderful manifestations are noticed, we find that men have not come into such close contact as to be rolled or fused into a compact mass. There, trees and plants, rivers and lakes, had ample opportunity to live in close relationship with men.

" In these forests, though there was human society, there was enough of open space, of aloofness ; there was no jostling. Still, this aloofness did not produce inertness in the Indian mind ; rather it rendered it all the brighter. It is the forest that has nurtured the two great Ancient Ages of India, the Vaidic and the Buddhistic.

"As did the Vaidic Rishis, Lord Buddha also showered His teaching in many woods of India. The royal palace had no room for Him ; it is the forest that took Him into its lap. The current of civilisation that flowed from its forests inundated the whole of India.

"The very word 'āranyaka' affixed to some of the ancient treatises, indicates that they either originated in, or were intended to be studied in, forests."

It is noteworthy that when the open-air forest Universities gave place to buildings, sites of Universities were selected for the beauty of their natural surroundings, and they were also set in great gardens, and spacious court-yards—the University of Vikramashilā had one which held 8,000 persons—added to the open-air character of the whole. A high wall surrounded such an abode, sometimes with only a single door, and a learned pandit was the door-keeper, who put the would-be student through an examination, ere he would open the door for his admission—a literal entrance examination, for the applicant could only enter when he had argued in satisfactory fashion with the door-keeper. I like to imagine a severe-looking pandit, squatting on the top lintel, and putting his head over the closed door, as he tries to outwit the eager yet anxious lad below, being in a rather unfairly superior position as he poses his questions.

The most ancient Hindu University, in the modern sense of the word, was Takshashilā (Takkashilā or Taxilā), which was destroyed by the barbarian White Huns in 455 A.D. How great its antiquity may be we do not know, but light may be thrown on this question as the excavations go on. It was situated some twenty miles on the north-west of the present town of Rawalpindi. Sir John Marshall, Director-General of Archæology in India, has given a most interesting account of its unburying, but he says regretfully:

> "The monuments of Taxilā were wantonly and ruthlessly devastated in the course of the same [fifth] century. This work of destruction is almost certainly to be attributed to the hordes of barbarian White Huns, who, after the year 455 A.D., swept down into India in ever-increasing numbers, carrying sword and fire wherever they went, and not only possessed themselves of the kingdom of the Kinshāns, but eventually overthrew the great empire of the Guptas. From this calamity Taxilā never again recovered."

Sir John Marshall published in 1921 a *Guide to Taxilā,* but he can only give us the bones of the wonderful University, whose life stretches far back into Hindu history. In the *Mahābhārata* we read that King Janmajaya conquered its valley and made there his great Snake Sacrifice; it comes into ordinary history only with its conquest by Persia B.C. 521, and by Alexander of Greece, B.C. 326. The King of the city makes submission to him, and we are told that it was then "very wealthy, prosperous and well-governed," and that its territory extended from the Indus to the Hydaspes. It is thought from some traces found in the excavations, that Apollonius of Tyana visited the city during his travels.

Its site carries out the idea held by the ancient Hindus of the value of natural beauty in the surroundings of a University. The valley is "a singularly pleasant one, well-watered by the river Hard and its tributaries, and protected by a girdle of hills." It was situated on the great trade route, which in those times connected India with Central and Western Asia, and Hiouen-Tsang, in the seventh century A.D., eleven hundred years later than the Persian conquest, found the valley still growing rich harvests and well-watered, but the University had perished two centuries earlier.

We can, however, reconstruct the outline of the living University from the Buddhist *Jātakas*, wherein we find no less than 105 references to it, showing how teachers and students lived in Ancient India, and the discipline imposed on the latter, sons of Kings and themselves future rulers though they might be!* *Jātaka* (No. 252) thinks that this discipline was likely "to quell their pride and haughtiness".

Professor Radhakumal Mookerji gives the following pleasant account from this same *Jātaka* as follows:

"Once on a time Brahmadatta, the King of Benares, had a son named Prince Brahmadatta. Now Kings of former times, though there might be a famous teacher living in their own city, often used to send their sons to foreign countries afar off to complete their education, that by this means they might learn 'to quell their pride and high-mindedness,' and

*I used in the sketch here given from my Convocation Address to the Mysore University, 1924, the six-volume edition "translated from the Pali by various hands under the editorship of Professor E. V. Cowell," and published at various dates. The numbers of the *Jātakas* are given, not the pages of the volumes, so that the references may be found in other editions.

endure heat or cold, and be made acquainted with the ways of the world. So did this King. Calling his boy to him—now the lad was sixteen years old—he gave him one-soled sandals, a sunshade of leaves, and a thousand pieces of money with these words: 'My son, get you to Takkasilā and study there.'

"The boy obeyed. He bade his parents farewell, and in due course arrived at Takkasilā. There he inquired for the teacher's dwelling, and reached it at a time when the teacher had finished his lecture, and was walking up and down at the door of the house. When the lad set eyes upon the teacher, he loosed his shoes, closed his sunshade, and, with a respectful greeting, stood still where he was. The teacher saw that he was weary and welcomed the newcomer. The lad ate and rested a little. Then he returned to the teacher and stood respectfully by him.

"'Where have you come from?' he asked.

"'From Benares.'

"'Whose son are you?'

"'I am the son of the King of Benares.'

"'What brings you here?'

"'I come to learn,' replied the lad.

"'Well, have you brought a teacher's fee, or do you wish to attend on me in return for teaching you?'

"'I have brought a fee with me,' and with this he laid at the teacher's feet his purse of a thousand pieces.

"The resident pupils attend on their teacher by day, and at night they learn of him; but they who bring a fee are treated like the eldest sons in his house, and thus they learn. And this teacher, like the rest, gave schooling to the Prince on every light and lucky day. Thus the young Prince was taught."

The learned Professor points out that :

"This extract introduces us practically to all the principal features of the education of the times. To go to Taxilā is 'to complete their education'. The appropriate age for the University was sixteen."

This age, as marking the beginning of the higher Education, has persisted to our own time, though now that a foreign Government controls Education, a later age is laid down.

"The Prince of Benares is . . . sent to Takkasilā for his studies with the modest equipment given him by his own royal father of 'a pair of one-soled sandals, a sunshade of leaves, and a thousand pieces of money,' as his teacher's fees, of which not a single pice could he retain for his private use. Thus the Prince enters his school as a poor man, divested of all riches."

The Professor says of the University :

"The fame of Takkasilā (Taxilā) as a seat of learning was, of course, due to that of its teachers. They are always spoken of as being 'world-renowned', being authorities, specialists and experts in the subjects they professed. It was the presence of scholars of such acknowledged excellence and widespread reputation that caused a steady movement of qualified students drawn from all classes and ranks of society towards Taxilā from different and distant parts of the Indian Continent, making it the intellectual capital of the India of those days. Thus the various centres of learning in the different parts of the country became affiliated, as it were, to the educational centre or the central University of Taxilā, which exercised a kind of intellectual suzerainty over the wide world of letters in India." (A paper in the *Vishva-Bhārati Quarterly*, October, 1923, p. 228.)

The sons of poor men who went as pupils helped in the cutting of fuel and other domestic services, or they promised to pay a fee later, either earning it, or begging for it. So honored was learning and so valuable to the country that to beg for it was no disgrace. Teachers less sought after taught without fee, and as we shall see, there were Universities supported by gifts from Kings or the wealthy, where teachers and pupils alike were boarded, fed and clothed.

As Professor Cowell says, the *Jātakas* are " full of interest as giving a vivid picture of the social life and customs of Ancient India. . . . They form in fact an ever-shifting panorama of the village life such as Fa-Hien and Hiouen-Tsang saw it in the old days before the Muhammadan Conquest, when Hindu institutions and native rule prevailed in every Province throughout the land." And what a wholesome, industrious, prosperous life it was !

The journey from Benares to Takshasilā was 2,000 leagues and dangerous when passing through a great forest, inhabited by "ogresses," but this passage was preferred being half as long as the safe way round (No. 96). A pupil is beaten for stealing sweets (No. 353). "A world-famed teacher preached the moral law to anyone that he might see. . . . But though they received it, they kept it not" (No. 356). Kshattriyas and Brāhmanas "came from all India to be taught the Arts" (No. 353), and one of these was archery (No. 374). Prince Junha of Benares, being in a hurry, accidentally knocked down a poor man and broke his bowl; he stopped and helped the man up, who asked for the price of a meal as his bowl was broken; the Prince said he had no money, but when he was King in Kāshi he would pay, and the man should come and claim his debt (No. 456). Outcastes were not admitted; but two who slipped in, disguised as Brāhmanas, were discovered by their use of bad language when, the rice being very hot, it burnt their mouths; they were beaten and driven away (No. 498). Good manners even under strain, were evidently insisted on. Professor Radhakumal mentions that Takshasilā had military, medical and law schools.

The extraordinary range of subjects taught in these ancient Universities is amazing, and the more so when we remember that a student was apparently expected, in many cases, to know by heart the book he studied. A Brāhmana learning one, two, or three Vedas, had to learn each by heart, and twelve years' study was assigned to each. Pandit Vasudeva

Sarvabhauma was the Head of the great University of Nadiyā, and it had no college for the study of the Nyāya philosophy. Only one copy of the text-book of Nyāya was extant, and that was in the possession of the University of Mithilā. This University refused to allow a copy of the book to be made, but Pandit Vasudeva was not daunted. He went to Mithilā as a student and learnt the text-book by heart. Then, going back to his own University, he opened a college for Nyāya!

In the *Chhāndogyopanishat* we are told that Nārada went to the Lord Sanat Kumāra and asked for instruction. The Supreme Sage asked him what he already knew, and Nārada replied:

"O Lord, I have read the Rigveda, the Yajurveda, the Samaveda, fourth the Atharvaveda, fifth the Itihāsa and Purāna, Grammar, Rituals, the Science of Numbers, Physics, Chronology, Logic, Polity, Technology, the Sciences cognate to the Vedas, the Science of Bhūtas, Archery, Astronomy, the Science of Antidotes and the Fine Arts." (These are said by Shrī Shankarāchārya to be the Science of making essences, dancing, singing, music, architecture, painting, etc.) "Unto him said Sanat Kumāra: 'All these that you have learnt are merely nominal.'"

The great University of Nadiyā in Bengal was founded about 1063 A.D. and still exists as a relic of the Past. In 1908 it had thirty Toles (Colleges) with 250 pupils, and the Toles still maintained the old custom of each teaching only a single subject.

Professor Cowell's visit to it in 1867 has been mentioned. Its old studies included the three (or perhaps four) Vedas, the Vedāngas, the six Darshanas, the Purva and Uttara Mimāmsa, Logic and Yoga. In the days of its glory, it was a town the life of which was devotion to learning. Mr. Shishir Kumar Ghose in his work, *Lord Gauranga*—Lord Gauranga was, as a youth, a student at Nadiyā, by name Nimai, and became later famous as Chaitanya, regarded by many as a minor Avatāra, an incarnation of Divinity—says:

"The intense devotion to learning by the majority of the citizens of Navadwipā [Nadiyā] gave a peculiar character to the town, distinguishing it from any other in the world. Students thronged everywhere. They filled the market-place, the streets, the bathing ghāts of the strand. They assembled in thousands in every convenient spot to hold literary discussions. When the students walked in the streets they talked on literary subjects. Literary tournaments were held every day at every ghāt of the city. And so earnest were the combatants that sometimes these tournaments ended in free fights, and the defeated parties had to swim across to the other bank of the river.

We must not omit to glance at a Southern Indian Institution, the only analogue of which I know is the modern literary body, the Académie Française. It was called the Sangam, a Tamil variant of the Samskrit Sangha. The word Sanghārāma is used for Buddhist monasteries, all of which included also schools, or colleges, or a University, the teaching being largely, though by no means entirely, in the hands of the monks, who were students as well as teachers. Professor S. Krishnaswami Aiyangar, M.A., Ph.D., a very high authority on ancient Tamilian institutions, tells us that there were three famous Sangams of Madura, each lasting through a long period of time ; he writes :

"There are two features with regard to these assemblies that call for special remark. The first, the academies were standing bodies of the most eminent among the learned men of the time in all branches of knowledge. The next, it was the approval of this learned body as a whole that set the seal of authority on the works presented to it." (*The Calcutta Review*, January, 1822, p. 43.)

This last point is my reason for comparing the Madura Sangam to the Académie Française, for the imprimatur of the "Forty Immortals" is regarded all over Europe as marking a book of exceptional merit. The books which received the approval of the Indian Sangam were known as "Sangam works," says our author, who writes as to the word that

"it means ordinarily no more than an assembly. In this particular application, however, it means a body of scholars of recognised worth and standing in the world of letters, who were maintained by the contemporary Kings, and constituted themselves a board, before whom every work seeking recognition had to be read. It is only when this body as a whole signified its approval that the work could go forth into the world as a Sangam work." (*Some Contributions of South India to Indian Culture*, pp. 9, 10.)

The highest honor given by the Madura Sangam was to tie a fillet round the head of some great scholar, and to place him on a platform furnished with poles, borne on the shoulders of learned men—one of the bearers sometimes a King—and thus carrying him in procession. Our Professor tells us that

"a Ruler of Tanjore, poet, musican, warrior, and administrator, did extraordinary honor to a lady of the Court, by name Rāmachandrāmha, who composed an epic on the achievements of her patron, Raghunatha Nayaka of Tanjore. It appears she was a poetess of extraordinary powers, who could compose with equal facility in eight languages, and was accorded the honor of Kanaka-Ratna Abhisheka (bath in gold and gems). She was, by assent of the court, made to occupy the position of 'Emperor of Learning'." (*Calcutta Review*, p. 49.)

In the Buddhist Period Nālandā holds the place that Takshashilā held in the Hindu. It was fully described by Fa-Hien, living in India from 399 to 414 A.D.; by Hiouen-Tsang, living there from 629 to 645 A.D., and by I-Tsing from 673 to 693 A.D., who out of these twenty years lived in Nālandā for ten. It was a great Buddhist monastery, founded by Āryadeva on a spot selected for its beauty on the banksof the sacred river, Gangā, by his Guru, the famous Nāgārjuna, and built up to extraordinary splendor by four successive Kings of Magadha. Mr. J. Talboys Wheeler wrote:

"The huge monastery was a vast University—towers, domes and pavilions stood amidst a paradise of trees, gardens and fountains. . . . Ten thousand Buddhist monks and novices were lodged and supplied with every necessary. All the inmates were lodged, boarded, taught, and supplied with vestments without charge. They studied the sacred books of all religions. In like manner, they studied all the sciences, especially arithmetic and medicine."

Hiouen-Tsang writes enthusiastically of the splendor of the architecture, the lakes of pure water covered with the blue lotus, and the "lovely kanaka trees." The library building had nine stories, and there were a hundred lecture rooms. Dr. Macdonnell remarks that in some subjects, "as Science, Phonetics, Grammar, Mathematics, Anatomy, Medicine and Law, the attainment of Indians was far in advance of what was achieved by the Greeks". (Quoted by Rao Sahab R. Krishna Rao Bhonsle, in *South Indian Research*, Jan., 1922.) Mr. Romesh Chandra Dutt, in his *Civilisation in Ancient India*, p. 127, writes:

"Buddhism had never assumed a hostile attitude towards the parent religion of India; and the fact that the two religions existed side by side for long centuries increased their toleration of each other. In every country Buddhists and orthodox Hindus lived side by side. Hindus went to Buddhist monasteries and Universities, and Buddhists learned from Brāhmana Sages. The same Kings favored the followers of both religions. The Gupta Emperors were often worshippers of Shiva and Vishnu, but loaded Buddhists and Buddhist monasteries with gifts, presents and favors. One King was often a Buddhist and his son an orthodox Hindu; and often two brothers followed or favored the two religions without fighting. Every Court had learned men belonging to both the religions, and Vikramāditya's Court was no exception to the rule."

Mr. Dutt quotes Dr. Ferguson as justly remarking that

"what Cluny and Clairvaux were to France in the Middle Ages, Nālandā was to Central India, the depository of true learning, the centre from which it spread over to other lands. . . . Medicine appears to have made great progress in the Buddhist Age, when hospitals were established all over the country. The great writers on Hindu medicine, Charaka and Sushruta, lived and wrote in the Buddhist Age, but their works seemed to have been recast in the Paurānic Age (p. 123). But it was in Astronomy that the most brilliant results were achieved in the Buddhist Age. We have seen before that astronomical observations were made as early as the Vaidic Age; and that early in the Epic Age the lunar zodiac was fixed, the position of the solstitial points marked, and other phenomena carefully observed and noted (p. 119)."

In the seventh century, the life of Nālandā seems to be deteriorating, if one may judge by I-Tsing's "laborious and minute work"—very tedious also, if one may venture to say so. I wrote on it elsewhere, that no one could read it

"without recognising that little attention was paid to the Lord Buddha's perfect Ethics and His superb Philosophy. I-Tsing's account is all about minute and mostly unimportant sittings and walkings and gestures. There is no life, no inspiration."

During the next century, Nālandā's place was largely taken by the Royal University of Vikramāshilā, which flourished for four centuries, and perished, with those of Nālandā and Odantapuri in the Muslim invasion of 1199. Two others were destroyed four years later, in the Muslim invasion of 1203.

In considering the destructive raids of the Muslims on these seats of learning, it is only fair to remember that even so fierce an assailant as Mahmud of Ghazni was a patron of learning in his own country. He had a fanatical horror of images, and as both Hindu and Buddhist Universities had Temples in their great gardens, containing images of Devas and of the Lord Buddha, and the country schools were also attached to Temples, these would share in the destruction launched against all "idols". The Musalmān, like the Hebrew, admits no images, whether of men or Devas in his architecture, and like the Puritan of the seventeenth century in Britain, he ruthlessly destroyed buildings which included them. And as, to him, learning was no excuse for "idolatry," he included monks and scholars in his wild rage.

After settling in Northern India for some time, this rage subsided, and Sultān Fīrūz, in the fourteenth century, began to tread a wiser way. He says:

"Among the gifts which God has bestowed upon me, His humble servant, was a desire to erect public buildings. So I built many Mūsjids (Mosques), colleges and monasteries, that the learned and the elders, the devout and the holy, might worship God in these edifices, and aid the kind builder by their prayers."

(The chief authority on Muslim Education in India is Narendranath Law, whose monograph, *Promotion of Learning in India During Muhammadan Rule (by Muhammadans)* is a most useful and interesting work.) He gives a pleasant description of the Madrasah (College) built by Sultān Fīrūz:

"The Madrasah was a very commodious building embellished with lofty domes and situated in an extensive garden, adorned with alleys and avenues, and all that human art combined with nature could contribute to make the place fit for meditation. An adjacent tank mirrored in its shiny and placid breast a high and massive house of study, standing on its brink. What a charming sight was it when the Madrasah hummed with hundreds of busy students, walking its clean and smooth floors, diverting themselves on the side of the tank, or listening in attentive masses to the learned lectures of the professors from their respective seats." (*Loc. cit.*, p. 60.)

A useful survival of Hindu-Buddhist methods was found at the Fīruz-Shāhi Madrasah, in the common life of professors and students, who all lived within the Madrasah itself, and each received a daily allowance for his maintenance. There was a large Masjid, in which the five regular hours of prayer were observed, and it is interesting to note that Sufīs conducted the regular compulsory prayers, so that they were evidently not then regarded as heretical. Travellers from distant countries also found hospitality there, and the poor and needy received charity.

Mr. Law also mentions that many small Muslim kingdoms sprang up in different parts of India, and that each contributed to the general progress of Islāmic learning, some being specially notable as centres, such as Jaunpur under its famous king, Ibrāhīm Shārgi. His daughter-in-law also built a Masjid, a College and a Monastery, and gave stipends to professors and students, and it is recorded that this institution had hundreds of subordinate ones, where also both professors and students were given stipends, "that they might devote themselves to learning in complete freedom from material needs and anxieties".

An outstanding lover of learning and pattern of toleration was the great Akbar (A.D. 1566-1605), who —in the period in which Catholic Mary burnt Protestants alive and Protestant Elizabeth crushed Catholics to death under heavy stones—held weekly discussions, in which "Sūfīs, doctors, preachers, lawyers, Sunnis, Shias, Brāhmanas, Jains, Buddhists, Charvakas, Christians, Jews, Zoroastrians, and learned men of every belief" argued on "profound points of science, the curiosities of history, the wonders of nature." Many translations into Persian were also made from Hindu Sacred Books, and Hindus and Muslims studied in the same schools.

Such was Education in India under Indian Rule, whether Hindu, Buddhist or Muslim. When that great bird of prey, the East India Company, winged its way eastward and descended on her land, ravaging and destroying, filling itself fat with ill-gotten spoil, Education naturally shared in the general ruin. Nearly a century after the Battle of Plassey, Sir Charles Wood (in 1854) by making a foreign tongue the medium of education, dealt the *coup de grace* to village education, the most potent creator of her wealth, the most vital element of her civilization.

For the great Universities—so inadequately described for want of space, given part of a chapter in a small book—were by no means the only glories of Education in India. To these, boys could be admitted, as said above, only after they had reached the age of sixteen, after their school education was over. In the very small villages the Temple priest acted also as school-master; the larger villages, like the towns, had also the Tole or the Madrasah, giving higher school education. Education began at five or six, and was continued in the village Toles and Madrasahs till the age of sixteen, at which it concluded, so far as its literary side was concerned. Apprenticeship to one or other of the skilled village trades must have run side by side with the later years of this. We have seen that every village had its school, and this meant that the whole country was educated, and explains how the East India Company obtained its scribes and accountants from the villages. The Village System had, in the course of ages, become a singularly perfect economic institution, with its various organs sustaining the common life. It was a body, an individual, organized for a rich and healthy life. It is now dying in a slow agony, for its education has been destroyed, its industries have been destroyed, its common property in its land has been destroyed (as we have seen in Chapter I); all that is left to it is agriculture, and man cannot live on food alone. He needs clothes, houses, tools, education, amusements. We have seen "The Present," as it affects the Village as a whole. Let us now watch the dissolution of its Education, the coming of the night of ignorance, where Light had once shone.

B.—The Present

India, once known over the world for her Education, whose Universities drew students from Europe to Asia, is now regarded as the most illiterate of civilised countries, with the possible exception of Russia.

This is not her fault.

Mr. Gokhalé, whose figures were dreaded by Indian officials because they could not deny their accuracy, and he used them with deadly effect in his attacks on British Rule, collected, in his efforts to obtain education for his fellow-countrymen, the following figures on the sums spent on education abroad :

" 16*s*. per head in the United States. In Switzerland, 13*s*. 8*d*. per head. In Australia, 11*s*. 3*d*. In England and Wales, 10*s*. In Canada, 9*s*. 9*d*. In Scotland, 9*s*. 7½*d*. In Germany, 6*s*. 10*d*. In Ireland, 6*s*. 5*d*. In the Netherlands, 6*s*. 4½*d*. In Sweden, 5*s*. 7*d*. In Belgium, 5*s*. 4*d*. In Norway, 5*s*. 1*d*. In France, 4*s*. 10*d*. In Austria, 3*s*. 1½*d*. In Spain, 1*s*. 10*d*. In Italy, 1*s*. 7½*d*. In Servia and Japan, 1*s*. 2*d*. In Russia, 7½*d*., and in India barely 1*d*."

In these figures lies the explanation of the change from what she was, of which the following samples may serve as evidence.

Mr. Keir Hardie's book, *India*, says :

" Max Muller, on the strength of official documents and a Missionary Report concerning Education in Bengal prior to the British occupation, asserts that there were then 80,000 native schools in Bengal, or 1 to every 400 of the population. Ludlow, in his History of British India, says that ' In every Hindu village which has retained its old form, I am assured that the children generally are able to read, write and cipher, but where we have swept away the Village System, as in Bengal, there the village school has also disappeared.' That, I think, disposes effectively of the boast that we are *beginning* to give education to the people of India."

The Court of Directors of the East India Company, in an exceptional moment surely, on June 3, 1814, stated in a despatch, referring to Village Communities and their schools:

"This venerable and benevolent institution of the Hindus is represented as having withstood the shock of revolutions, and to its operation is ascribed the general intelligence of the natives as scribes and accountants. We are so strongly persuaded of its great utility that we are desirous you should take early measures to inform yourselves of its present state and that you will report to us the result of your enquiries, affording in the meantime the protection of Government to the village teachers in all their just rights and immunities, and marking, by some favorable distinction, any individual amongst them who may be recommended by superior merit or acquirements; for, humble as their situation may appear, if judged by a comparison with any corresponding character in this country, we understand these village teachers are held in great veneration throughout India." (Quoted by Mr. Matthai, *loc. cit.*, p. 43.)

It would have been difficult to find "in this country" any "corresponding character," since, at the time of this despatch, English villagers were notoriously ignorant of writing, there not being in every village a schoolmaster. However, three years later, the East India Company, the lucid moment having passed, destroyed the Village System in which the village schoolmaster had his place. The cultivators who had had shares in the common land were turned into rent-paying peasants by a tax on their holdings, and could not afford to pay a schoolmaster in their impoverished condition ; so, very few schools survived. Now, in 1926, a child, whose parents wish to have him educated, may have to walk in the morning seven miles to the nearest school, and seven miles back in the evening—a somewhat heavy addition to the day's work.

The crimes of the East India Company were many and grievous ; but perhaps of them all, this light-hearted destruction of India's Village System, by plunging a rich and educated country into frightful poverty and into illiteracy, must be held to be the blackest.

Mr. John Matthai, in his *Village Administration in British India* (Chap. II, p. 42), says :

" It is obvious that when the British took possession of the country, in the different Provinces they found that, though in most parts of the country except Western and Central India, there existed a widespread system of National Education, so far as they could trace, the position of the schoolmaster had in many cases changed from that of a village servant with a defined position in the community into that of a casual worker—honored in the village by reason of his sacred calling, but not sufficiently identified with the village to hold his ancient place on the village staff. This statement is true in the main, but nevertheless there were various traces left which pointed to the original connection of the school-master with the village economy."

One other corroboration of the general education prevailing in the country may be quoted with the unimpeachable authority of the *Encyclopædia Britannica* behind it (see under "India," p. 384, column 1):

"At no period of its history has India been an altogether unenlightened country. The origin of the Devanāgari alphabet is lost in antiquity, though that is generally admitted not to be of indigenous invention. Inscriptions on stone and copper, the palm-leaf records of the temples, and, in later days, the widespread manufacture of paper, all alike indicate, not only the general knowledge, but also the common use of the art of writing. From the earliest times the caste of Brāhmanas has preserved, by oral tradition as well as in MSS., a literature unrivalled alike in its antiquity and in the intellectual subtlety of its contents. The Muhammadan invaders introduced the profession of the historian, which reached a high degree of excellence, even as compared with contemporary Europe. Through all changes of Government vernacular instruction in its simplest form has always been given, at least to the children of respectable classes, in every large village. On the one hand the Toles, or seminaries for teaching Samskrit philosophy at Benares and Nadiyā, recall the schools of Athens and Alexandria; on the other, the importance attached to instruction in accounts reminds us of the picture which Horace has left of Roman education. Even of the present day, knowledge of reading and writing is, owing to the teaching of Buddhist monks, as widely diffused throughout Burma as it is in some countries of Europe. English efforts to stimulate education have ever been most successful when based upon the existing indigenous institutions."

The change has come quickly, for a generation or two, left uneducated, present a picture of illiteracy. Yet evidently some struggle was made to retain knowledge, for Mr. Adams, in an enquiry into the number of Hindu and Musalmān schools in the Bengal Presidency, 1835-1838, reported that there were Toles and Madrasahs "in all the larger villages as in the towns". "The curriculum," he said, "included reading, writing, the composition of letters, elementary arithmetic and accounts, either commercial or agricultural or both." How rapidly Muhammadan education is decreasing appears in the *Quinquennial Review* for 1907 to 1912. In 1907, there were 10,504 "*Quran*" schools as compared with 8,288 in 1912; in 1907, there were 2,051 Arabic and Persian schools, as compared with 1,446 such schools in 1912.

The Great Universities reacted on the villages, for we have seen that Princes having finished their Education in these, visited the Villages in order to see that the artificers kept up to the traditional level in their artistic work.

The present state of Education is the more poignant

	1919-1920.	1920-1921.	1921-1922.	1922-1923.	1923-1924.
Total population	244,020,100	244,834,626	247,097,651	247,103,887	247,107,341
Number of boys in public primary schools	4,956,988	5,117,219	5,111,850	5,379,621	5,690,820
Number of girls in public primary schools	1,176,533	1,210,754	1,198,550	1,220,495	1,264,814
Percentage of boys in public art colleges, high schools, primary schools, to the male population	5.1	5.1	5.04	5.26	5.7
Percentage of girls in public art colleges, high schools, primary schools, to the female population	1.1	1.1	1.12	1.14	1.9
Total scholars in public institutions	7,612,839	7,774,993	7,742,225	8,178,975	8,674,003
Percentage of total scholars to population	3.36	3.42	3.39	3.48	3.77

because of its terrible contrast with the glorious Past. Statistics are said to be dry, but they are the strongest argument in this case for Indian control over the Indian land. Let me put the figures bluntly, for they are their own strongest indictment of British Rule where Education is concerned. (Education, as a subject is, since 1921, under an Indian Minister, but he is restricted by the inadequacy of the funds allowed to him and cannot recast the system until the whole Government is Indian.) But, in their very first Provincial Councils, the members passed a measure for Free Education in seven Provinces out of eight—or out of nine, if Delhi be counted as a Province—and in four of these Compulsory Education was also passed ; in the other three, compulsion was to be introduced as soon as possible without dislocating labor, child labor being so largely employed.

Such is the state of Education in India after 167 years of the blessings of British Rule. Perhaps, without over-harsh criticism, one may say that, as regards Education, British Rule is inefficient.

In the Indian States the figures are very different, approaching more nearly the old level. In Baroda, Education is Free and to a great extent Compulsory, all boys going to school. In Travancore 81 per cent. of boys and 33 per cent. of girls are at school. In Mysore 46 per cent. of boys, but only 10 per cent. of girls.

This is what England has done for Education in India. India's patriots have done what they could to induce the Indian Government to spread Education. Mr. Gokhalé pleaded for popular education, but was met with the answer, "No money." There was money enough for the Army; the ever-rising military expenditure was never checked for want of money; against that no argument as to the poverty of the people availed. The extravagant expenditure on British soldiers was never restricted for want of money, but popular Education was evidently regarded as a mere fad of the "natives". Moreover it was dangerous. England had discovered by her own experience that as "the working classes" became educated, they interfered more and more in political affairs, and were more and more impatient about the existence of a highly privileged class, talked of land nationalisation, of shifting the heavy burden of taxation to shoulders more able to bear it, and of other dangerous changes. Could then anyone in his senses wish to see the manual workers of India educated? In the small number of the educated Intelligentsia lay the safety of the alien Rule.

But even that small number was too many for Lord Curzon, while Viceroy of India. Indian lads have a passion for education, and little as they know of their own Past, their inborn craving for education is unconquerable. Of this I have had a large personal experience as President of the Governing Body of the Central Hindu College and School for eighteen years, and later of the Theosophical Educational Trust. I have known boys walk literally hundreds of miles, begging their way, to reach the above School, and to all arguments as to "no room," "we cannot take more free scholars," such a one would only answer: "Mother, you *must* teach me." The old traditions still hold of the *right* of the boy to education. Lord Curzon's Universities' Act of 1904 was designed to increase the control of Universities by the Government and also the cost of University Education. It aroused the bitterest opposition, and his name is still hated in India because of it, for scholarship and wealth have not been generally united in the India of the Past. Long before Lord Curzon had struck his blow at University Education and closed it to large numbers of the class with whom learning was a traditional right, we have seen that Sir Charles Wood, just fifty years before the University Act, had made popular education impossible by making English, a foreign tongue, the medium of instruction in schools. He also invented a new type of University, which destroyed it as a Temple of Learning, and made it into a mere examining body. Such were the eccentricities of modern foreign officials, pitchforked into the Government of an ancient and civilized people, of whose traditions they were utterly ignorant. Some of them meant well, doubtless, but the proverb proved to be true, that "hell is paved with good intentions".

Sir Charles Wood's curious experiment of educating the professional classes in a foreign tongue—as though Eton and Harrow boys were taught exclusively in German—not only tended to de-nationalize them, but closed to them the history of their own country; for its history, as taught in the Government Schools, was written by an Englishman, leaving them to grow up ignorant of the fact that they were heirs of a Past unparalleled in history; it also offered them knowledge which they could not assimilate, because they were struggling to follow the language while they should have been grasping the facts. Their only resource was to utilise their extraordinary power of memorising by learning text-books by heart and reproducing them in the examination-room. We hear sneers about "Bābu English," when a young man writes an application for employment in the language of Addison; but the critic forgets that *his* Nation is responsible for the peculiar "education" imparted to the youth.

A still more serious injury was done to the Indian people by imposing "English Education" in a mutilated form; for it was devoid of the religious and moral training, which in England formed an essential part of it. The "English-educated" were practically left without religion or ethics during the most impressionable period of their youth, and materialism consequently spread over the land; the home was fortunately kept free from it, for the women of India were untouched; but a dangerous gulf was dug for boys and men between the home life and the outside one; the husband could no longer be his wife's true companion in her religious life, and her religion, full of devotion, largely lost the elevating effect of knowledge; for the husband was ignorant of his ancestral faith, and the religion of the home became a matter of ceremonial, while the meaning and use of this were no longer understood. The son, studying in an English school and college, was less careful than the father in avoiding injury to the feelings of his feminine relatives, and distressed them by questions they could not answer and by indifference to that which was dearest to their hearts. Hence the delight with which they welcomed the Central Hindu School and College, and the gifts of Indian women formed no mean portion of its income.

One good thing, however, English Education has done, though its good results were unintended—and were by no means welcome when they appeared. It gave to Indian youth the history of England, with its struggles for Liberty, its revolutions, its literature, full of inspiration for Freedom ; it gave India Milton, Byron and Shelley ; it taught how the American Colonies became the American Republic. English-educated India, small in numbers, caught the infection of English patriotism, learned to admire England as the citadel of Freedom, and rejoiced to hear how that little Island became the refuge of Kossuth, of Mazzini, of Russian Terrorists, to read how Garibaldi, the Liberator of Italy, was welcomed in London as he passed through streets packed with crowds, shouting their delight that Bomba's tyranny was overthrown, mad with enthusiasm for the red-shirted soldier who had set his country free. Strange that a Nation, which was ruling autocratically over another People, should thus dig the grave of its own despotism. Out of all the plundering merchants who had swept into India and fought out their quarrels on her soil, *that* one was chosen as her temporary Sovereign under whose rule, as I once pointed out, India's Freedom, her winning back of Self-Rule "was inevitable". English Education was to awaken India to a sense of her own humiliation. It was the destined destroyer of her subjection.

I once more quote what I have written elsewhere of the mixed results of English Education in India:

"When Macaulay urged English Education, he was looking down with contempt on the great literature of India, and did not realise that, in pressing English Education, he was condemning to ignorance the great masses of the people. Instead of bread he offered a stone. Boys were brought up without any knowledge of the Classics of their country. They could declaim in English, but not in their mother-tongue. There is no subtler way of denationalizing a country than to make the language of the upper classes, of the Law and the Courts, of the Colleges, a foreign tongue, and to require a knowledge of the foreign tongue for Government Service. The Brāhmanas took advantage of these conditions and crowded the Law Colleges, the Medical Colleges, the Secretariat. The higher class Non-Brāhmanas, landlords and merchants chiefly, learnt their own language, but, with the Muslims, did not trouble themselves much with the foreign tongue. Hence they became technically 'backward classes,' and have only lately begun to covet Government appointments."

Let me remark here that it is interesting to note that England largely, though not entirely, followed in her educational policy that of Russia in Poland. The Polish language was forbidden in schools, and Russian was the language employed just as English is employed here. Autocracies of all Nations must resemble each other.

" Yet English Education did just what was wanted —corrected India's excessive deference for ' lawful authority ' ; its literary masterpieces in defence of Liberty, in denunciation of tyranny, added to the persistent harping of their teachers on the blessings of British Rule, led to the re-awakening of the ' ineradicable love of Liberty of the Āryan peoples,' and of a desire to have the blessings of British Rule by sharing in it themselves. Thus came into existence the ' educated Indians,' the now detested ' Intelligentsia,' a small minority, but the hope of their country. And those who hate them and denounce them do not realise that, for Indians, they are not a separate class ; they are closely tied up with the village folk, the villagers are closely related to them ; what the Intelligentsia think to-day, the villagers think the day after to-morrow. Hunger is a severe but effective schoolmaster, and the villagers have long memories of what their forebears were before the village freedom was destroyed, and the village schoolmasters disappeared."

And hunger is increasing, as we have seen.

C.—The Remedy

Once more we must look to our village as the basic element in the remedy for the present state of Education. As will be seen by turning to Chapters IV and V, " The Awakening of India " and " Home

Rule for India," the Commonwealth of India Bill places Education in the hands of the Pañchāyat, the Sabhā, the Samiti and the Provincial Legislative Council. The Village Pañchāyat controls Primary Education and Village Workshops and Libraries. The Taluka Sabhā controls Lower Secondary or Middle Schools and Model Farms. The District Samiti controls Higher Secondary or High Schools and Colleges, Technical Colleges and a Technical Institute (for the study of soils, manures, crops, etc.). The Provincial Legislative Council, Universities, Technical Institute (including research, agricultural education, protection against destructive insects, pests, plant diseases), Libraries, Museums, and Zoological Gardens.

It will be observed that Literary, Arts and Crafts, and Technical Schools and Colleges run side by side all the way up. That is, the scheme provides for a good general education, but also trains eye and hand and, later, branches of scientific and technical equipment along specialised lines.

Objection is raised to the cost of education. Of course, if a Government insists on brick buildings, and tables and benches and expensive apparatus and blackboards and slates, etc., etc., the expense is crushing. But our Village Pañchāyat will do nothing so foolish. Most of the year the children can have their classes in the open air, as they do now in our village schools (unless we want Government grants). In the rainy season a shed of bamboo-supports and palm-leaf thatch suffices. They learn writing by smoothing out sand and making letters with a pointed stick. They learn the multiplication table by heart up to 20 × 20. They sit on the ground, much more comfortable than if they sat on a bench, with their little legs dangling. They sit on the ground at home, why not at school?

With this there must be manual training, Montessori for the little ones, carpentry, spinning, weaving, agriculture, for older students. The carpenter's shop makes the apparatus for the small people; the spinners and weavers make cloths; vegetable and flower gardens lead up to agriculture. Geography is taught by clay and sand models, beginning with the school building, marking out houses, roads, well, temple, etc. History by stories. Religion and morals are taught first by stories, and above all by example, and by helping each other in little acts of service. The Scout movement supplements the school classes, and both make the future good citizen. Up to seven years of age we train the senses chiefly, and see that every child has enough simple and suitable food; from seven to fourteen the emotions chiefly; after fourteen hard mental study and plenty of team games. I am not speaking here from theory, but from twenty-eight years of practice in India.

The useful *Madras Bulletin of Co-operation* tells us of Japanese education (Japan has village, sub-district and district elected councils); that in 1904 Japan had 27,138 primary schools, with 108,000 teachers and above 5,000,000 pupils; in the higher primary lessons are given on plants and animals, bearing on agriculture, horticulture, and local industries. After this come the secondary schools, agriculture taught practically, "chemistry and physics, diseases and pests affecting the crops"; the normal schools have a four years' course of agriculture and "a full year of special agricultural work in the College of Agriculture in Tokio". Experimental and demonstration farms were being established.

All this is very encouraging, when we see that the Japanese have a local government such as we are striving for here, and also that they are eastern people. A Government of India note says of the Indian peasant:

> "Owing partly to historical causes and partly to the fearful struggle that has to be carried on with nature in many parts of India, the Indian cultivator has, as a rule, developed into the most patient, hard-working and in many cases skilful agriculturist that can be found on the face of the earth."

After all, history tells us of him for thousands of years, and he was only entirely deprived of his freedom and his communal system of land-holding a century and a decade ago. The memory of it remains. It is capable of revival.

In the Secondary Schools, the vernacular should be the sole medium of instruction, so that the students can follow the language through which knowledge is communicated to them. English should be taught as a second language. It should be taught at first by conversation and then modern English stories, and poems, and simply and graphically written English history; the high schools should have for reading, essays by the best writers, writers of exquisite prose such as Ruskin, of inspiring ideals, such as Emerson, histories, great poems, biographies of really great men, not of admirals and generals of foreign Nations.

With full command of modern English, with taste formed, and interest aroused, they will be ready for the intelligent study of the great masterpieces of English literature of the sixteenth, seventeenth and eighteenth centuries.

What after all is the object of Education? To train the body in health, vigor and grace, so that it may express the emotions in beauty and the mind with accuracy and strength. To train the emotions to love all that is noble and beautiful; to sympathise with the joys and sorrows of others; to inspire to service ever widening in its area, until we love our elders as our parents, our equals as our brothers and sisters, our youngers as our children, and seek to serve them all; to find joy in sacrifice for great causes and for the helpless; to feel reverence for all who are worthy of it, and compassion for the outcast and the criminal. To evolve and discipline the mind in right thinking, right discrimination, right judgment, right memory. To subdue body, emotion, and mind to the Spirit, the Inner Ruler Immortal, making the mind the mirror of the Ego, the emotions the mirror of the Intuition, the body the expression of the Will.

To put all this in a single sentence: To make the man a good Citizen of a free and spiritual Commonwealth of Humanity.

III

INDUSTRIES

A.—Their Past

WE have seen that India was, and still is, a country of villages, not of towns. We have also seen that the sons of the learned, the royal, the noble, and the wealthy merchant classes, "the twice-born," highly trained in the Universities, were there instructed in the Fine Arts and Crafts, and that they visited the villages, whence their wealth was drawn, utilising their knowledge for the inspection of the Village Industries, thus maintaining the high level of the craftsmen, while they also drew to their palaces or their homes artists of genius, maintaining them freely and leaving them the fullest liberty to produce their works at their own time and in their own way, being content to reap their own reward in the fame and the glory which accrued to them from the presence of such men of artistic genius in their Courts or in their homes.

I mentioned in the Introduction the large and lucrative trade of India with foreign countries, noting that whenever foreign visitors left records of their observations, they wrote of the wealth of articles produced by her craftsmen, and her great export trade, bringing streams of gold into the country, enriching her merchants. We saw that it was this trade with Babylon, Nineveh, Egypt, Persia, Greece and Rome and continuing in Europe and the Far East down to the seventeenth century A.D., that drew to her the trading companies of Europe and reduced her to poverty. On this there is no question possible; hence we can deal very shortly with this part of our subject.

These companies obtained charters from their respective monarchs to plunder India, and none of them made any pretence that they went to India for her salvation, to lift her out of chaos, and give her the blessings of peace and order—see Lord Sydenham's articles *passim*. They were quite frank as to their object, and if proof were needed the despatches of the East India Company to their representatives in India may suffice. They came to "shake the pagoda-tree," a vegetable that has become quite barren now. And as India was a country of villages, they sought the splendid products of village looms and exported them, to reap enormous profits. When these began to fail by the destruction of the village system, they built large factories and employed cheap labor. This was the "absentee capitalism"—like the "absentee landlordism" of Ireland—whereof Gokhalé spoke, when President of the National Congress of 1906, as draining the land of wealth, declaring that in the preceding forty years it had amounted, including treasure, "to no less than a thousand millions sterling." We shall come presently to the means employed.

I wrote elsewhere in dealing with this modern flight of locusts—of which it might be said that "the land was as the Garden of Eden before them, and behind them a desolate wilderness:

"They came to a land overflowing with gold and silver brocades, carpets of silk and gold, tufts of gold for turbans, golden network. An Emperor had a throne of the estimated value of £6,500,000. There were works of art of every description, muslins wonderful for fineness, as well as the calicoes, so valued in England. The huge fortunes obtained by men like Clive, who 'wondered at my moderation,' all told of a country wealthy beyond compare, and wealthy with her own constantly manufactured articles, ever renewed and replaced as they were exported. And we can trace this continuous wealth back and back for millennia. India was never found poor until she reached the nineteenth century A.D. (The latter half of the eighteenth century would be more exact, as the process took time.) As Phillimore wrote in the middle of the eighteenth century, 'the droppings of her soil fed distant regions,' while she clothed in gorgeous garments the Doges of Venice, the great nobles of Italy, the Monarchs of Europe, century after century. Look back over the evidence of travellers who recorded what they had found. Travellers in the sixteenth, fifteenth and fourteenth centuries, mention with admiration her manufactures, her trade and the fertility of her soil under irrigation, in some parts yielding three crops a year. At the end of the thirteenth century, Marco Polo records a similar story: indigo, pepper, ginger, cotton, surplus rice were exported, as were buckrams, fine in quality, leather goods, beautiful mats. Similar testimony is found back and back, and Pliny in the first century speaks of the great trade of Rome with India, Arabia and China, and the wares being sold at a hundred times their cost."

We learn from Bernier, in the seventeenth century, that one Bengal village, Kasimhazar, was exporting annually 2,200,000 lbs. (of 16 ozs. to the lb., notes a writer) of silken goods. The old skill has not wholly disappeared, though now rare. Even now in Benares, we may watch a weaver in a little hut, large enough to contain his loom and himself, producing one of the exquisite silken fabrics for which that city of immemorial antiquity is famous. Or we may listen in Masulipatam, in Southern India, as a man chants an ancient melody, and several weavers, with threads of various hues, reproduce the notes he sings in a harmoniously hued pattern for a coat of many colors.

There are still a few centres of highly skilled work, as in Benares and Masulipatam. When the Queen-Empress visited Benares she bought many of its still wonderful products; golden scarves—now called Queen Mary's scarves—others colored, but with glimmering sheen of gold shining amid the color; sārīs with borders of golden work woven in—literal gold, which keeps its threads bright under many washings through many years, not the imported "gold thread" which soon loses its brilliance. These hand-woven fabrics last for years, and remain beautiful. In far Kashmir shawls are still made of exquisite colors, the shades so delicate and so marvellously graded that we cannot see a dividing line with European eyes, though at one part the color is deep and after awhile light; sārīs warm and soft, but so fine that they will pass through a woman's ring. The best kinds are dying out, as the old purchasers of such goods can no longer afford to buy them, or in some cases, I fear, men of wealth or young Princes prefer to gamble on horse-races and other western delights, rather than to support the arts of their native land.

A few other places remain, bearing witness to the splendor of the Past, but they too are lessening in number. Many of the Industries perished with the Education, which the villagers could not support when the Village System was destroyed, and the Village Community no longer owned the land on which it lived, and on which it carried on its varied inter-dependent occupations, agricultural and industrial.

As Europeans are fond of writing about the continual wars in India causing insecurity and poverty, it is well to point out, as previously stated, that the fighting in Āryan India was confined to the military caste, and travellers have noted and recorded this fact. The villages, as the sources of wealth, were respected. The invaders from the countries north of the Indian boundaries were sometimes devastators, like the White Huns, but more often carried off with them on their return home only the most easily portable plunder, like jewels, of which astonishing amounts are said to have been annexed. But the loss of jewels does not seriously impoverish a country depending for its food on home-grown crops, and for other necessaries and for trade on its "unrivalled skill in manufacture," of which Sir Thomas Munro spoke in 1813. The early Musalmān invasions destroyed Temples and Monasteries and slaughtered their inhabitants—learned men and scholars—and probably killed many who resisted; but the area they covered was proportionately small, and Mr. Matthai relates how the inhabitants of a devastated village would return and rebuild their houses and take up again their avocations. In the late War, the parts of Belgium and France invaded and occupied by German troops are rapidly recovering, and neither is in a "state of chaos," though the War was more destructive and cruel than any war which preceded it. At the worst, the state of India compared with that of contemporary Europe was less disturbed by wars, while it never suffered from an Inquisition, nor did India ever expel many thousands of useful citizens, as Spain expelled the Moors and the Hebrews, destroying herself in the process.

The general security of life and property is reported by travellers at periods when many dangers to both were found to exist in countries outside her well-ruled and prosperous area. We read also of numerous banks, a well-known sign everywhere of security and settled government. I have already mentioned the fact, showing the normal high level of integrity prevailing among the people, that written receipts were not given for money or valuables deposited for safe keeping. British Rule introduced a new standard, making the honest return of money or goods dependent upon the depositor possessing a written receipt, acknowledging the deposit; the Court refused to compel the return unless the depositor presented the written receipt. A double standard of honesty was thus introduced by British Courts; a man's word no longer bound him; he might cheat a depositor by retaining his property, unless the latter had demanded and obtained a written receipt for it; if he had followed the rule of honor prevalent in his own country before the advent of the English merchants, British Justice sanctioned his dishonesty—one of the many evil results of foreign rule, where the foreigners are not only ignorant of the customs of the people they govern, but also look down upon the people as inferior to themselves, look upon their customs with contempt, and force their own upon them.

We must turn to the present and see how it came about, and why the craft of hand-weaving fell on evil days. It was partly due to deliberate wickedness, inspired by selfishness and greed, and partly to the closer contact with the West, the increased facilities of transport and communications, and the consequent competition of power-machine-made goods. Mr. A. Ranganathan remarks, in the pamphlet before quoted:

"In Madras the number of people supported by industries fell from 5,591,058 in 1911 to 4,112,771 in 1921. Mr. C. W. E. Cotton, Director of Industries, finds it difficult to suggest any adequate explanation for the fall. And yet the explanation seems to me simple enough and it may be summed up in two phrases: Lack of discriminate encouragement of the home industries and unfair competition from outside."

B.—The Present

We have shown that India was a country of Industries; but of Village Industries, not of factories; of handicrafts, not of power-machinery. These industries were part and parcel of her Village System, and their decay has been the financial ruin of India. No country can be prosperous which depends entirely on the raw products of its soil; crafts must flourish as well as agriculture, and from their union is born prosperity. It will be remembered that it was the destruction of the wool industry of Ireland by Britain that drove half her people from her shores as emigrants to the United States of America, and compelled many of those left behind to go as laborers to England during the harvest season to supplement, by the wages there earned, the poor living which they could gain in their own land. Here in India the story has been repeated on a huge scale, and the peasants, averse to emigration, starve at home, while many migrate to towns during the slack season, when women and children suffice for the agricultural work. Moreover, the destruction of Village Industries has had an indirect result, aggravating agricultural difficulties. Many craftsmen, especially the weavers, unable to dispose of their wares and unable also to face the competition of the cotton cloths of Lancashire, deserted their ancestral craft and took up poor land on the margin of cultivation, yielding poor crops.

As Mr. Ranganathan remarks:

> "This unceasing pressure on land has resulted in more and more land being brought under cultivation, and people are finding it increasingly difficult to support themselves by agriculture. In the very nature of things in India, there are at present, few ways by which the agriculturists can supplement their income by subsidiary activities of one kind or another."

Lancashire was further aided to supplant India-woven fabrics by the astounding policy of Britain, which taxed Indian-produced cloth for the benefit of the Lancashire products, imposing what was called the Cotton Excise; she protected Lancashire imports against the competition of home-made cloths, taxing Indian products so that Lancashire might compete with Indians in India "on equal terms"! It was Protection upside-down. Very different had been English policy when the production of Lancashire cotton mills was in its infancy. Indian calicoes were highly valued, as we have seen, by Englishwomen, who preferred them to those of Lancashire. So a duty was levied on all imports of such goods. As this did not suffice for the shutting out of the superior Indian wares, an Act was passed forbidding their import, and the import and selling of such goods was made a legal offence. After a time, the Indian trade with Britain was killed, and Lancashire, having mastered the English market, then demanded the opportunity of supplanting Indian industry in India. The Cotton Excise imposed on Indian goods supplying the Indian market was then invented, and was only abolished last year, despite its scandalous and unique injustice. And this after, be it remembered, the open unabashed plunderingof the eighteenth century, the impoverishment of India going hand-in-hand with the rise of English industrialism. As Lecky said in his *History of England in the Eighteenth Century* :

"At the end of the seventeenth century, great quantities of cheap and graceful Indian calicoes, muslins and chintzes were imported into England, and they found such favor that the woollen and silk manufacturers were seriously alarmed. Acts of Parliament were accordingly passed in 1700 and 1721 absolutely prohibiting, with a very few specified exceptions, the employment of printed and dyed goods of which cotton formed any part."

Indian Industries were, in this way, aided by heavy import duties on other Indian products, practically destroyed. England was then in favor of Protection for her own nascent industries, becoming a Free Trade country only when she had a surplus to export, and when "the great Dependency" was becoming an agricultural country only. Mr. A. Ranganathan writes on this :

"The iron industry of the country was similarly

killed. Captain Townsend of the ordnance department has left it on record, that India is more richly endowed than any other country in iron ore, and this is confirmed in the observations to be found in one of the statistical Atlases of India published under the authority of the Government in the eighties. When the Government decided to establish a system of railways, they might have simultaneously attempted to manufacture the necessary iron out of the ore available in India, and had it at a less cost than they paid to get it from England. This would have, according to Mr. Ball, Deputy Superintendent of the geological survey, kept vast sums of money in circulation in India and given employment to large numbers of people who, for lack of it, were obliged to swell the ranks of those dependent on land, to the inconvenience of all, for their livelihood. The same fate as befell the cotton manufactures overtook the once thriving shipbuilding industry of India. Mr. Taylor in his *History of India* has the following—

"'The arrival in the port of London of Indian produce in Indian-built ships created a sensation among the monopolists, which could not have been exceeded if a hostile fleet had appeared in the Thames. The ship-builders of the port of London took the lead in raising the cry of alarm; they declared that their business was on the point of ruin, and that the families of all the shipwrights in England were certain to be reduced to starvation.'

"And an obliging Government saw to it that the Indian industry perished."

The Insurance Companies have frustrated attempts to revive it by refusing to insure the sailing craft used for coastal transport because they do not use steam. And when some Bombay and other merchants some years ago floated a company for passengers going abroad, it was opposed by a combination of rival English Companies and was unable to succeed.

The policy of the East India Company was to reduce India to the condition of a "plantation," that she might supply English manufacturers with raw materials, receiving a portion of them back as manufactured articles, while the price of the home-made cloth was increased by the cotton excise.

Following the same policy, attempts have been made to force Indian cultivators to grow long-stapled cotton, suitable to the factory machinery, instead of the short-stapled, which suits the hand loom, the kind of cotton they are accustomed to cultivate. In concessions for mining minerals, for fresh land, for wood for manufacturing purposes, Indians find themselves everywhere handicapped in their own country, and see the foreigner preferred.

In 1912-13, we find from the Government figures of exports that raw materials and produce and articles mainly unmanufactured (coal, gums, resins, lac, hides and skins, metallic ore, scrap iron or steel, oil-seeds, tallow, wax, textile materials, woods, timber, etc.), were exported to the value of Rs. 1,030,479,594. The value of textile cotton manufactures imported was Rs. 608,215,774.

The condition of the weaver is rendered terribly difficult by the same burden as presses on the agriculturist—the burden of hopeless debt. He gets yarn, or the money wherewith to buy it, from the money-lender, and one condition is generally made, that he sell his cloth to the money-lender at a price less than the weaver could gain in the open market. In other cases the money-lender is the owner of a number of looms, and lets out looms to weavers on hire, repaying himself by paying each weaver a price below the value of the cloth produced. The weaver thus becomes a wage-earner instead of an independent earner of his livelihood, a free man, while the money-lender becomes a small capitalist, accumulating the profits over subsistence wage of the men whose labor he buys. This system is utterly alien from Indian thought, and if it spread widely would bring about only a repetition of the factory system, already started in India by foreigners, the "absentee capitalists" of Mr. Gokhalé, and copied, in self-defence, by a number of Indians. If this spreads, India will have to go through the capital and labor struggles of the West, with all their evils, their hatreds and their extremes of wealth and poverty, which have culminated in the present terrible strike in England, and the, for the moment, abortive general strike. It means a state of social war, which will lead to future general strikes till the system perishes, and co-operation succeeds competition. There are signs of the coming changes in the United States, where Trade Unions are taking over productive enterprises and creating their own banks.

The Madras Government has endeavoured to help the weavers by sending round a demonstration party to teach them the use of the fly-shuttle by which the productive power of the weaver is much increased. A Weaving Institute was also started in the midst of a weaving district. In Bengal, again, 10,000 weavers were trained in a weavers' Training College, and then returned to their villages to teach others.

Mr. E. B. Havell, the author of *Artistic and Industrial Revival in India*, has been a persevering worker in the task of saving the Indian Weaving Industry. He says in this work :

" But do not let it be supposed that the mechanical improvements necessary for the continued existence of India's greatest industry are mainly a matter for expert knowledge. They are a few simple things, which any intelligent school boy or girl could learn to manipulate in a week, though they are so important for the village weaver that were the Education Department as efficient as it should be, every village schoolmaster would teach them and every Inspector of Schools would be able to demonstrate them. Possibly some day a Director of Public Instruction may come to realise this but, having vainly hammered at official doors for many years, I cannot waste much more time there. It is, after all, more important that India should learn the lesson of self-help.

" These suggestions apply to the village weaver who is too poor, helpless, and ignorant to make any attempt to adopt even the simplest improvements to his apparatus. The educational measures hitherto employed, officially and unofficially, hardly touch his case at all. It is useless to provide schools, exhibitions and demonstrations of improved appliances for his edification. He cannot afford to leave his loom to attend them and has not the means, even if he had the energy, to obtain the required improvements which might help him out of his difficulties; though the cost of them would seem to be a small matter, for a total expenditure of ten or twelve rupees would provide him with apparatus which would certainly double, and, in some cases, treble his output (pp. 177, 178).

"I have several times called public attention to the success which Mr. A. F. Maconochie, I.C.S., had, while he was Collector of Sholapur, in the Bombay Presidency, in reviving the local weaving industry by the simple expedient of making arrangements to provide the weavers with raw materials on reasonable terms, advancing them cash at reasonable rates in the slack season, and enabling them to obtain the best market price for their labor—all of which advantages are denied them by the rapacious village money-lender. In three years the condition of three hundred weavers had greatly improved, twenty-five of them had paid off all their old debts, and recovered their mortgaged property from the sowcars; and at the same time the scheme itself had given a fair dividend on the capital used.

"If this can be done without any attempt to improve the methods and appliances of the weavers, it stands to reason that an efficient organization which gives both financial and practical educational assistance would be certain of success. The example of ten thousand weavers in the Serampore District of Bengal is a proof that simple improved appliances can enable village weavers to double their earnings even without any outside assistance (pp. 179, 180)."

In India, of late years, another road has been taken, which, with Home Rule, will succeed far more rapidly than it can hope to do under a foreign Government, and against the opposition of the foreign capitalists, with whom the few large Indian capitalists are associated. The Madras Government also has tried to revive the weaving industry through co-operation, but its suspicions of the capacity and honesty of Indians, unless supervised by the English, cripples the co-operative side of the revival, on which widespread success depends. The suspicion is absurd, comparing the Past of India with that of Britain. It is easy to employ Indians in subordinate positions wherein they deny them all initiative, and then to declare that they have none; Indians can only show their powers where they are free, and the millennia of their prosperous Past compared with their condition under British Rule is the answer. It is true that where the British force their own ways on the Indians, the latter often do not work them well, having had no training in them. For instance, Local Self-Government in the Districts and sub-Districts is often complained of, but where, as in Bengal, the Act instituting local Government has been framed more on Indian lines, it has been a great success, as has been shown in the third Section of Chapter I.

This other road is that of co-operation, the institution of Co-operative Banks and Village Co-operative Credit Societies. In the Annual Report of Co-operative Societies in Bihar and Orissa, 1911-12, we find the following:

"Experience has proved that a co-operative society well formed and properly supervised can be run by ordinary villagers with immense benefit to all concerned. It can save the raiyat from the mahajan and give him a new outlook on life; it can make him thrifty, hard-working and self-reliant; it can improve agriculture, sanitation and education; it can heal factions and stop petty litigation; it can make village life healthier in all its relations. All these results I have myself seen. Of all the methods of attacking the agricultural problem, not on one but on every side, co-operation is incomparably the most promising. A net-work of societies would immensely facilitate general administration, for the principle goes to the very root of the matter. The instinct of association is already deeply implanted in the people, and the co-operative movement which appeals primarily to this instinct has undoubtedly come to stay."

In the *Madras Bulletin of Co-operation* many useful figures are given to show the spread of this movement. It was practically started by the Act of 1904, and by 1912 there were 957 Co-operative Credit Societies in Madras Presidency, and the Central Urban Bank had deposits from these to the amount of Rs. 2,443,370.

Such Societies not only aid weaving but all agricultural and other industries.

It is probable that such activities would be far more successful if built on the lines of the old Craft Associations, some of which still survive, as the goldsmiths, and those of master builders, masons and decorators, who lately built the splendid palace of the Mahārāja of Mysore.

In connection with Industries, many western writers refer to the Guilds in India, and in a very useful lecture given by Mr. M. R. Sundara Aiyar, under the auspices of the Indian Guild of Science and Technology, he laid much stress on the old Crafts of India. I have not seen the lecture itself, but only a long report in the Allahabad *Leader* (a daily journal, edited by a learned and brilliant Indian, Mr. C. Y. Chintamani). The following summary will show its drift. Mr. Sundara Aiyar compared the Indian Guilds with the Mediæval Craft Guilds of Europe, but pointed out that they worked in harmony with the Government of the kingdom in which they were, not against it, as often in mediæval European countries. He noted that while in Europe these Guilds were oppressed by the robber Barons, who were then so numerous—who came down upon the Guilds to take away their wealth, as they grew wealthier and wealthier by their industry—the Indian Guilds themselves often served as Municipal Councils, and in large centres the headsman of each Guild was represented in the Council. They were thus linked up with the Government here instead of being in opposition as they were in Europe. The lecturer urged that these methods of local administration, which had existed from the remote past in India ought now "to be developed in two directions: firstly, in developing the present municipal organization of the country, which would maintain its branch railways, minor irrigation works, roads, police, institutions for primary education, sanitation, and for the relief of the poor" and so on; secondly, "in the productive and distributive, co-operative and profit-sharing industrial associations, which would organize capital and labor efficiently for the welfare of the community". He rightly pointed out that:

"the promulgation of wrong theories as to ancient Indian polity and the relegation of India to the primitive stage of civilization, have led many to argue that Indians were not familiar with constitutional forms of government, or Self-Government, and many Indians themselves have come to believe in that theory."

Surely because their "English Education" had not included the study of Indian history as given in their own literature. They knew the City State of Aristotle the Greek, but not the Village Republics of Kautilya. Mr. Sundara Aiyar criticised the evidence of *Indian* witnesses before a Royal Commission, that Indians were not fit to be heads of offices or Directors of Companies. He rightly said that the study of Indian Mediæval Guilds discloses a remarkable development of municipal organization and corporate industrial life. He described the regulation of wages, the collection of rates and taxes, and the system of local finance with which these local bodies were able to carry on the administration without much help from the central Government.

I do not myself think that the local Village Pañchāyats and the Craft Guilds were identical, except perhaps in very small villages. We have to remember that village government in ancient times, while stable in essentials was adaptable in non-essentials; in large villages there were quarters assigned, as we have seen, to different trades, while in small ones no such aggregations took place; the rules of each Craft, derived from its Shilpa Shāstra would be customary, "what always has been," and these Guilds would be spread over large areas, while the Village Pañchāyat was concerned with Village Administration; here again, in small villages they might take counsel together, while in large each would have its own Pañchāyat. The duties mentioned above are concerned with Village Administration, not with Craft Rules.

C.—The Remedy

As has already been said in Section (*B*) some efforts have already been made to revive the Village Industries by improving the looms of weavers, and by Co-operative Credit Societies and Co-operative Banks. When Self-Government is restored to the Villages, these methods will receive an immense impetus, though they can never be completely successful until the old balance of agriculture and industries is restored in every village, and until the other crafts for the supply of necessaries in the village are also re-established, such as the iron-smith, the carpenter, the potter, the spinner, for the local supply of yarn, and until the communal holding of land replaces individual peasant-proprietorship, and the old system of pasture and forest is restored. This will entail village shepherds and wood-cutters. The Co-operative Society will have among its workers the agent for the collection of surplus products and their transfer to towns for sale, and to agents in ports for export abroad. It will probably be found convenient to have distributive stores in Taluka towns and in the District capital, to lessen the work of the village agents. But these details will be arranged by business men, and need only be outlined here.

Among the powers given to the Village Pañchāyat, in the Commonwealth of India Bill, are the establishment and control of Co-operative Stores and Banks, as well as of Cottage Industries, so that the villager can dispose of his products at the Stores within the village itself; these form the first link in the transfer chain which unites the producer to the port for export after the home market has been fully supplied. The reader will see why I have emphasised Village Self-Government as the basis of all effective reforms in the political field. No foreign official, trained in the ways of the English market supplied with factory-made goods, can adapt himself to this immemorial way of working of the Indian. As this system becomes complete and all its parts are fitted together, forming a complete whole of industrial production and distribution, I doubt very much whether the factory system will be able to hold its own in India, a country of villages; then we shall get rid of the crowded slums in the few factory towns, the nests of diseases and of the appalling infant mortality; the babes will be born in healthy conditions, will grow up, as their ancestors did, in healthy surroundings, will receive education as of old, will have free, wholesome, well-fed, happy lives.

Far-sighted Indians among the Intelligentsia are recognising this. Here is an extract from the lecture before quoted of an Indian gentleman, now Sir C. P. Ramaswami Aiyar, speaking many years ago to a District Conference, the lecture issued as the pamphlet, *Co-operative Societies and Pañchāyats*:

"The one method by which this evil (emigration to towns) can be arrested, and the economic and social standards of life of the rural people elevated is by the inauguration of healthy Pañchāyats in conjunction with the foundation of Co-operative Institutions, which will have the effect of resuscitating village industries and of creating organized social forces. The Indian village, when rightly reconstructed, would be an excellent foundation for well-developed co-operative industrial organization."

Again:

"The resuscitation of the village system has other bearings not usually considered in connection with the general subject of the inauguration of the Pañchāyat System. One of the most important of these is the regeneration of the small industries of the land. Both in Europe and in India the decline of small industries has gone on *pari passu* with the decline of farming on a small scale. In countries like France, agriculture has largely supported village industries, and small cultivators in that country have turned their attention to industry as a supplementary source of livelihood. The decline of village life in India is not only a political, but also an economic and industrial problem. Whereas in Europe the cultural impulse has travelled from the city to the village, in India the reverse has been the case. The centre of social life in this country is the village, and not the town. Ours was essentially the cottage industry, and our artisans still work in their own huts, more or less out of touch with the commercial world. Throughout the world the tendency has been of late to lay considerable emphasis on distributing and industrial co-operation, based on a system of village industries and enterprise. Herein would be found the origins of the arts and crafts guilds and the garden cities, the idea underlying all these being to inaugurate a reign of Socialism and Co-operation, eradicating the entirely unequal distribution of wealth amongst producers and consumers. India has always been a country of small tenantry, and has therefore escaped many of the evils the Western Nations have experienced, owing to the concentration of wealth in a few hands. The communistic sense in our midst, and the fundamental tenets of our family life have checked such concentration of capital. This has been the cause for the non-development of factory industries on a larger scale."

In small western countries, like Denmark suppremely, Co-operative Societies are successfully at work, both in agriculture and industry. Co-operative Dairy Farms export large quantities of butter, while Co-operative Industries form part of the village life. In Switzerland, village industries are found, and the handicrafts of Norway and Sweden are well known. Before the Russian Revolution, a great Russian woman, Mme. Pagotsky, brought over to England beautiful embroideries of Russian peasants, and other products, and established in London a centre for this sale. There are no cases, I think, of prosperity in village life in which the people have been thrown entirely on the land. Ireland, on a small scale, India on a large, have demonstrated by famine the hopeless misery of a population dependent wholly on agriculture.

As I have said above, the establishment of the rural Co-operative Credit Societies began only with the Act of 1904. Yet I find from *The Leader*—the Allahabad journal before mentioned—that Sir Edward Maclagan stated, speaking in 1913 to the Imperial Council, that, since 1906, the number of such Societies had increased from 843 to 8,177, and the number of members from 91,000 to 403,000. He also stated that large provincial Banks had been started in several provinces, and the capital at the disposal of the Societies had risen from Rs. 23½ lakhs to Rs. 235 lakhs (a lakh is

100,000). The *Madras Co-operative Bulletin* states that "in 1908 there were 1,201 Village Banks with a membership of 93,200, and 149 Urban Banks with 55,000 members, carried on upon co-operative lines". A year later there were 2,008 banks and 184,897 members.

The work of the Co-operative Societies, I may say in passing, should not be restricted to industries, for through them the Taluka Sabhā should purchase agricultural machinery and loan it to villages where the land needs deep ploughing and by communal holding is in sufficiently large areas, and should also have well-bred bulls to be loaned to villages to improve the breed of cattle where it is deteriorating.

With regard to the weaving industry, the Rev. J. H. Macfarlane says:

"There was one industry of supreme importance, namely, weaving. The multitude of hawkers at Kodaikanal provide an illustration *à propos*. Silks, fine and coarse cloths, rugs, curtains, and so forth were manufactured largely in villages. But one can never find a rich working weaver. All are poor for one or more reasons. What methods for the amelioration of the condition of the weavers could be emphasised by Missionaries? Firstly, improved methods of work should be encouraged and taught. The fly-shuttle should be introduced, where practicable. Secondly, a cheap machine is needed for preparing the warp. Thirdly, the weavers should be delivered from the middlemen. Few weavers are independent and they lose much by borrowing. Fourthly, the weavers should be urged to combine and co-operate in work and form weaving societies, to buy their own yarn and machines. But Co-operation is foreign to India, and this phase of work will be difficult to introduce."

This is quoted from a paper by the Rev. J. H. Macfarlane, of the London Mission, Cuddapah. He was speaking at the Missionary Industrial Conference. The last sentence is curious and has not been justified by events.

Along this road revival may be made while the political battle is going on.

IV

THE AWAKENING OF INDIA

WE have seen the unexpected result of English Education in India—the creation of what a Viceroy called a "microscopical minority," the English-educated Indians, the Intelligentsia of India. We have seen that, in India, the villages and the towns occupied to each other a position the reverse of that occupied by their congeners in the West. Separated in the West, they were closely blended in the East, and the members of the highly educated professional classes constantly speak of "my village," the village whence they came, the village of their ancestors. However slowly, the thoughts of the educated filtered into the villages and awoke in the peasantry the slumbering memories of their immemorial Past. They cared little for the politics of the towns, still less for those of Provinces, and of Governments yet further off—these had not affected seriously the "little village republics"; but they cared profoundly for their own village politics, which had been crushed half a century before. Under the influence of those who had made in 1884 the scheme of the National Congress in Madras, and had brought it into being in Bombay in 1885, the peasants began to discuss their grievances, and later to meet in conferences among themselves; vernacular newspapers, edited by one of the Intelligentsia, slowly reached the village, and a villager, able to read, would be surrounded by his fellows and read out the contents, to start fruitful discussions. News of outer doings passed from village to village in the strange eastern way, and the thought atmosphere changed. The ever-present teacher of hunger and suffering applied the lessons, and traditions became inspirations. Thus was the seed in the villages sown which sprang up as the agitation for Home Rule in 1915, when Mr. Gandhi said of myself: "She has made Home Rule a mantram in every cottage." The movement seemed sudden and surprising, because the seed was quietly sown. India's Intelligentsia worked to educate their countrymen, and the annual meetings of the National Congress, reported in the Indian Press, were as the rain falling on the hidden seed.

Meanwhile the movement for National Education was teaching patriotism and pride of race and country, aided by the spirit of Freedom breathed through English literature, as already said. The movement for National Education was its child. It began by lectures about 1895. The founding of the Central Hindu College and School at Benares in 1898, in which Hindus and Englishmen worked as professors and masters side by side on subsistence wages, in thorough equality, was followed by other institutions, inspired by a similar spirit; girls' schools followed under the same inspiration, and religion became an integral part of the training of patriotic youth, while the story of India's Past fired their enthusiasm. Religious Reform had led to Educational Reform, and Social Reform followed in their wake.

The work went steadily on, stimulated by the tyrannical policy of Lord Curzon, the Viceroy. We have seen his Education Act of 1904. The partition of Bengal fired that Province to fury and caused a total withdrawal of patriotic Bengalis from contact with the British autocracy. The elders stood coldly aside; the young plunged into a widespread revolutionary movement; Surendranath Bannerji, the "uncrowned King of Bengal," became the idol of the Province, Arabindo Ghosh its inspiration, intensified by his martyrdom. Gokhalé as President of the Congress of 1905, denounced the Viceroy; Dadabhai Naoroji, President in 1906, struck the note of Self-Government as the remedy.

"The whole matter can be comprised in one word, Self-Government, or Swarāj, like that of the United Kingdom or the Colonies . . . Self-Government is the only and chief remedy. In Self-Government lie our hope, strength and greatness. . . . Be united, persevere, so that the millions now perishing by poverty, famine and plague and the scores of millions that are starving on scanty subsistence may be saved, and India may once more occupy her proud position of yore among the greatest and civilized Nations of the West."

Another great figure had arisen in Indian politics, a statesman and a combatant against autocracy of the most militant type, Bāl Gangādhar Tilak. He inherited the fiery traditions of his race, the Marathas, strong-brained, strong-armed, that warred against the great Mughal Empire, and, had India been awake, he might have played the part of a Cromwell. He was imprisoned unfairly, and was only the more loved, and came out of gaol a bitter enemy of the British Rule. "Freedom is my birthright and I will have it," was his war-cry, and he aroused a spirit that will never disappear till Freedom is won. Two parties developed in Indian politics, embodied in the two great leaders: Gokhalé who would use only constitutional means, Tilak who would use constitutional or unconstitutional to set India free. India was then in the grip of a number of laws that made all effort to win Freedom dangerous. No man's liberty was safe who desired Freedom for his country. Men of the highest character, if they were known to desire a change in the methods of Government, were ordered to give security for good behavior, like vagabonds, and refusing, were thrown into prison. Gokhalé, with his small but splendid "Servants of India Society," the members of which were pledged to a life of poverty and political work, became the nucleus of the "Moderate," later the Liberal, Party, Tilak of the "Extremist". Tilak was again thrown into prison with a savage sentence of six years, to come out aged but unchanged in thought and courage. Meanwhile India had grown.

The Russo-Japanese war, a war between East and West as it was felt to be, was another element, this time from outside, which helped to awaken India, and was, from one point of view, her salvation. For Indian Ideals were in peril for the first time in her history, and Indian Ideals were essentially the Ideals of the East. The peril lay in the fact that she had assimilated all other invaders and had re-made them into Indians, but the British were denationalizing her by forcing on her their ways, their methods, their civilization, and were teaching her western-educated class to copy them and to regard their own as inferior. They could never be assimilated, for they were birds of passage, not settlers in the country; they carried "home" their gains from Indian cheap labor, and their pensions for having governed India inefficiently. So incessant was their insistence on their stay here as foreigners, that some Indians caught the ridiculous habit of saying, "I am going home this year," when they were going to pay a visit to England. The defeat of the great Russian Power by little Japan sent a shock of astonishment through India. What? An Eastern Nation facing a Western Nation on a field of battle? What? The white people were not then resistless? They had been met and overthrown by a colored race, by men like themselves? A thrill of hope ran through Asia, Asia invaded, Asia troubled by white "spheres of influence," with settlements of white people, insolent and dominant, rebelling against Eastern laws, rejecting Eastern customs with contempt, humiliating colored Nations in their own lands and arrogating powers to which they had no right. Despair changed into hope. Asia awoke, and with Asia India.

The hope strengthened when the new King-Emperor and his Consort visited India on their Coronation and when the Partition of Bengal, declared so often to be irrevocable, was revoked.

This act of justice taught India that, deprived of arms as she was, she was yet strong, even when all seemed hopeless, though the brutal methods of repression, the sufferings endured by her self-sacrificing youth, aroused a deep and abiding hatred, which dug a gulf between the Bengalis and the English rulers, and was the parent of later revolutionary movements in that Province.

In a lecture delivered in 1913, I laid down the views on which my whole work in India has been based: "the building up of India into a mighty Self-Governing Community"; "the old system of Government in India, more than any other, showed a genius for Self-Government in the people; it shows that the Indian, as it were by nature, is capable of guiding, of shaping, of controlling his own affairs. Competent Self-Government, effective Self-Government, can only be carried on over an area where the people who compose the governing body understand the questions with which they have to deal."

I submitted:

"The ancient system prevalent here dealt with things in a much more practical way, a way which made Self-Government at once effective, competent and real. If the Future is to be built on the Past, then we must have the Village Councils, the 'grouped Villages' Councils, and so on in extending areas to the District and Provincial Councils or Local Parliaments, and above them the National Parliament, which would send representatives to the Imperial Council. None would be without a share in governing, but his power would be limited to the area over which his knowledge extended, and there would be no barrier anywhere to the rising of the competent."

These are the principles which, twelve years later, were embodied in the Commonwealth of India Bill of 1925, now before the House of Commons in the British Parliament, ordered to be printed after it had passed its first reading. It was drawn up by the National Convention of 1925, of which I was General Secretary. The definite campaign for Home Rule began in the spring of 1914, on January 2, when my fellow-workers and myself started a weekly Review, *The Commonweal*, on the four lines already laid down. We stood for Religious Liberty, regarding all religions as ways to God; for National Education, "with an open path from primary schools through higher schools to the Universities"; for Social Reform, including foreign travel, uplift of the submerged classes, abolition of child-marriage, seclusion of women, color bar and the caste system.

The Political Reform we aimed at was Self-Government for India, in union with Britain in a spirit of love and co-operation, and we asked for this in the Home Rule League of 1915, the Congress League scheme of 1916, the Montagu-Chelmsford Reforms of 1919, the working them, unsatisfactory as they were, and the opposition in 1920 to Mr. Gandhi's Non-Co-operation movement.

Here is the declaration in *The Commonweal*:

"In Political Reform we aim at the building up of

complete Self-Government from Village Councils, through District and Municipal Boards and Provincial Legislative Assemblies, to a National Parliament, equal in its powers to the legislative bodies of the Self-Governing Colonies, by whatever name these may be called ; also at the direct representation of India in the Imperial Parliament, when that body shall contain representatives of the Self-Governing States of the Empire. All measures that tend in this direction we shall support, and all that retard it we shall oppose. We shall recognise the National Congress and the non-official members of representative bodies as voicing the will of India. We claim an open path for Indians to every post in their native land, as promised by the Proclamation of 1858, and the abolition of every law that places them in a position inferior to that enjoyed by the English. We ask that capacity and high character shall determine all appointments to office, and that color and religion shall be entirely disregarded as qualifications.

" One thing that lies very near to our hearts is to draw Great Britain and India nearer to each other by making known in Great Britain something of Indian movements, and of the men who will influence from here the destinies of the Empire."

In February, 1914, a heavy blow was struck at the movement for Freedom. Gopāla Krishna Gokhalé passed away. His right hand man, V. S. Srinivāsa Shāstri, was elected in his place, and nobly has he filled it ever since. Resembling his Chief in wide knowledge, steadfast devotion to India, calm judgment and polished eloquence, he has served his country well. Outstanding have been his services to Indians abroad in pleading for justice to them, and one great triumph has been the passing of an Act in Australia which has placed resident Indians on a perfect equality with the white Australian citizen, giving them all the same rights and privileges.

In the spring of 1914 I went to England, to try to form an Indian party in Parliament: the effort failed, but outside Parliament it was decided to support India's definite demand for Home Rule by forming an auxiliary Home Rule League for India, and at a crowded meeting in Queen's Hall, London, Earl Brassey in the chair, I urged the necessity of Home Rule, and in answer to an absurd suggestion that India's loyalty to British Rule must be "unconditional," declared that "the price of India's loyalty is India's Freedom". Mr. Jinnah and Lālā Lajput Rai supported the demand. On my return to India I bought a daily paper in Madras, published it on July 14, the date of the fall of the Bastille, and renamed it *New India*. Round this and the weekly *Commonweal* was destined to rage the battle for Home Rule against the use of the tyrannical Press Law (abolished by Reformed Councils in 1921 with a mass of other cruel legislation, including the Rowlatt Act), and they bore aloft the banner of Home Rule through the years of the Great Agitation which ended in 1917, when Britain declared her goal to be the establishment of Self-Government in India.

In the following month, August, 1914, came the

unexpected crash of the Great War. India at once recognized that the success of Germany would mean an Empire of Force, while the success of Britain would mean ultimately an Empire, or rather a Commonwealth of Free Nations, each Self-Ruling and acknowledging as their link a constitutional Monarch. She rose in defence of that Ideal, led by her Intelligentsia, forgetting all her sufferings. Practically the whole of the younger Bar of Madras volunteered to serve; the offer was rejected and a chill was felt, but a Madras Hospital Ship was equipped, the country villages sent their men, the rich their money. The lessons of the War began.

Things were said by leading British statesmen, two of them Prime Ministers of the Empire, which rang through India and have never been forgotten. Mr. Asquith drew a vivid picture of the condition of Britain if Germany should win the victory, if Germans ruled in Britain, levied taxes, held all highest offices, made her laws, controlled her policy; he passionately cried out that it would be "inconceivable and intolerable"; he spoke of the "intolerable degradation of a foreign yoke". Mr. Lloyd George declared that the principle of Self-Determination must be applied "in tropical countries". Later, President Wilson proclaimed that the war was to make "the world fit for free men to live in"—the world, not only Europe and North America. Was it any wonder that India recognised the world-humiliation imposed on her by her being ruled by a foreign Nation, of being subject to what had been described as the "intolerable degradation of a foreign yoke"?

She believed that all the fine phrases were true, and that she was fighting for her own liberty as well as for Britain's. Her army, kept on a war footing, was the first to reach the field of battle, was flung across the road to Paris on which the Germans were advancing, forcing back with their huge numbers the splendid but small army of Britain's veterans, who fought every yard of the way but inevitably fell back slowly before the great waves of Germany's overwhelming numbers. It was at that critical moment that the Indians arrived, and it was no wonder that in both Houses of the British Parliament the members sprang to their feet and cheered with hot enthusiasm, when the news reached them that the German advance was checked, and that the Kaiser's boast that he would "dine in Paris in a fortnight" had been falsified by the appearance of the Indians. General Sir James Willcocks, K.C.B., G.C.M.G., K.C.S.I., D.S.O., LL.D., who wrote a book, *With the Indians in France,* prefaced it: "To my brave comrades of all ranks of the Indian Army I dedicate this book, which is an earnest endeavor to record their loyalty and imperishable valor on the battlefields of France and Belgium." It was published in 1920, and Sir James spoke of what he knew, for he commanded the Indian Army Corps for a year, "for the first time in history to be employed in Europe". He ends the Introduction of his book, having said that it was due to India that the facts should be told, by writing:

"The day is past when that great portion of our

Empire could be kept in comparative darkness; the light is dawning, and the Great War has opened to her an opportunity which she never had before. Her sons have shared the glory of the Empire. From the boggy fields and trenches of Flanders and the desert sands of Egypt; from the immortal heights of Gallipoli; from the burning plains of Mesopotamia and the impenetrable jungles of East Africa, comes up with one voice, from the thousands who fought and bled for England:

"India has taken a new birth;
The heavens above, the sea, the earth
Have changed for aye, the darkness dies,
Light has illumined all men's eyes,
Since Armageddon's day. .

". . . . One of my chief difficulties at the beginning of this war was to make it understood that the Indians cannot be treated as pure machines, and that they possess national characteristics as varied as those between Scandinavians and Italians. I own that Sir John French and his Staff generally made every allowance for these facts, but there were others who made none; an Army Corps (no matter its fighting strength in numbers) was an Army Corps and nothing else. An Army Corps was supposed to be able to occupy so many thousand yards of trenches, and the orders were issued by this routine rule.

"It might be said the Indian Corps was sent as a Corps, and times were too pressing to go into such details; this is perhaps true, and we all recognised it at the beginning of the Flanders fighting; but as time went on and the German attack was beaten off, I saw plainly that you cannot expect a ship to keep up full steam when the engineers and stokers are lying shattered in the hold. And yet those brave men not only filled a big gap in our battered line, but, helped and encouraged by their comrades of the British battalions of the Indian Corps, held it against incessant attack. Minewerfers, hand grenades, and high explosives tore through them and flattened out their trenches; blood flowed freely; but as often as they were driven back from their defences they managed to return to them again. India has reason to be proud of her sons, and their children may well tell with pride of the deeds of their fathers."

Aye, that will be. But with it does go and will go the bitter knowledge that the men did not win liberty for their Motherland, and that instead of Freedom as the due recompense for all her sacrifices, India received the massacre of Amritsar and the ghastly atrocities under martial law in the Panjāb. And she remembers that she is still a subject Nation, and that such crimes are still possible.

In estimating the effect of the War on India, it must be remembered that the survivors returned to India at its conclusion; that they carried into the villages from which they came the story of their experiences, told how they had marched and ridden through London streets, packed with cheering crowds, had been fêted, honored by white people. They had proved themselves in the trenches side by side with white troops; the bodies of their comrades who had died to defend Britain were left in foreign lands. Was it wonderful that Indians began to say that they had been found worthy to die for the liberty of Englishmen, to share with England in deaths, wounds, hardships of every kind; they returned to their homes to find still pressing on their people and on themselves "the intolerable degradation of a foreign yoke".

The Indian National Congress of 1914 claimed "the recognition of India as a component part of a Federated Empire, in the full and the free enjoyment of the rights belonging to that status". That was the note that rang through India, and will ring until she wins Self-Rule. It repeated the note of the Congress of 1906, the note of Self-Government, Home Rule. Its policy was that all our strength should be turned into a demand for Home Rule, after gaining which all the piecemeal reforms we needed could be made by ourselves.

V

HOME RULE FOR INDIA

EVENTS moved fast. The Congress of 1915 ordered its Committees to prepare a scheme outlining India's claim. It was done and was endorsed at Lucknow by the Congress of 1916, and also by the Muslim League. Two Home Rule Leagues had been formed in September, 1916, and these worked side by side, and the two Presidents, Mr. Tilak and myself, were members of both. Enthusiasm had risen higher and higher, guided by a vigorous propaganda of pen and tongue during the autumn of 1915 and the spring of 1916, and the Madras Government took fright. Lord Pentland, the Governor, a kind and well-meaning but weak man, wholly in the hands of the old type of Civilians, allowed some of these to ally themselves with some of the ablest of the non-Brāhmanas to misrepresent the Home Rule Movement as the attempt of the small number of Brāhmanas to tyrannise over the huge majority outside their own caste; by utilising religious feeling to stimulate political ambition, these Civilians and the non-Brāhmanas formed an unholy combination which threw itself against Home Rule. The Government consequently thought itself strong enough to attempt repression, and the Press Act of 1910, which placed every newspaper in a Province at the mercy of the local Government, was used against *New India*, the leader of the Home Rule agitation. On May 26, 1916, a notice was served on myself levying a security of Rs. 2,000 on the paper. It was paid, and Lord Pentland and his Government became the chief propagandists of Home Rule, for *New India* continued cheerfully on its path, knowing that it was virtually doomed, unless the country rose in its defence.

Now came in the value of my political training by Charles Bradlaugh. "In fighting a bad law," he would say, "never give way, but utilise every opportunity of delay which the law gives you. For time is on the side of a just agitation, and stirs up the people." Little chance of delay was there in action taken under the Press Law, for it was by Executive Order to a magistrate, and the magistrate was bound to obey. Still the battle could be fought in the same spirit, fought out step by step, undeterred by inevitable failure. And it was so fought.

The security was forfeited on August 28, and a new security of Rs. 10,000 was levied. The Press Act gave to the Editor the option of paying in cash or in Government notes, but the Government of Madras did not feel bound by the law it utilised, and insisted on cash. The Law Officer of the Governor-General's Council had promised that interest should be paid on any security levied. The Madras Government taking cash, paid no interest, so levied also a continuing fine. I began an action against the Government for the interest, but that disappeared in the course of the struggle and the final triumph.

The Press Act was so worded that defeat was apparently certain, so beginning with a Special Bench in the Madras Court on September 27, 1916, I fought on up to the Privy Council. The Advocate-General of the Madras Government was the prosecutor and I defended myself, aided by the very able advice, and on a technical point by the skilful pleading of Mr. C. P. Ramaswami Aiyar. As I knew that I was bound to lose the case, I arranged to sell the *New India* Press, and the Vasanta Press on which also security of Rs. 5,000 was levied as the printer of the *Commonweal,* to two different persons when the need arose, as the next step of the Government, under the Act, would be to forfeit the Presses. I was wholly acquitted under the charge of sedition and was admitted to be perfectly loyal to the Crown; but some of the articles were held to come under other all-embracing sections of the Act, so drawn that, as Sir Lawrence Jenkins, the Chief Justice of the Calcutta High Court, had pointed out, no one attacked by the Executive under it could possibly escape. As time was wanted, I applied against the decision of the Madras Court to the Privy Council, as that prevented the Government from taking further action until the appeal was decided. The Government, having levied a second security could not forfeit it and then forfeit the Press, until the case had been decided in London—a way of fighting that had apparently escaped the notice of the Government of India in its efforts to strangle the Indian Press. It had many successes with papers not trained, as I had been, in the way of fighting bad law legally. Charles Bradlaugh had abolished securities on the English Press by the policy he had recommended to me in case of need, and had received John Stuart Mill's congratulations thereon. He must have been pleased, I think, when the first reformed Legislative Assembly and Council of State, abolishing a mass of "emergency legislation," reduced the Press Act to an innocuous Registration Act.

A Home Rule (English Auxiliary) League had been formed in England in 1915, in aid of the Indian Movement, and it re-published a little book of mine, entitled *India—A Nation*, when the English Government, in 1916, persuaded the publishers to withdraw it from circulation.

The adoption of the "Congress League Scheme," mentioned above, gave fresh vigor to the agitation, and this so provoked Lord Pentland, that he told the Madras Legislative Council (May, 1917) that "all thoughts of the early grant of Responsible Self-Government should be put entirely out of mind". It was apparently decided by the Madras Government that as *New India* went on with the propaganda of Home Rule, and as it could not forfeit the security and then the Press, because of the appeal to the Privy Council, it would stop the paper by interning the Editor (myself), the Assistant Editor (Mr. B. P. Wadia) and a particularly breezy and popular contributor (Mr. G. S. Arundale), by interning this most objectionable trio. These three out of the way, the paper would probably collapse. The order was issued on June 16, no reason being given, and Lord Pentland refusing any explanation though he called me to see him—why or what for, I never learned; he may have supposed I would take the opportunity of asking for mercy, but I did not. As I wrote a little later:

"I suspended *New India* on June 18th, sold the Vasanta Press to Rao Sahab G. Soobhiah Chetty and recovered its Rs. 5,000 on June 19; on June 20, I sold the *Commonweal* Press to Mr. Ranga Reddi and the *New India* Press to Mr. P. K. Telang, recovering Rs. 2,000 and Rs. 10,000, and issued a notice to *New India* subscribers; the paper appeared again on the 21st; it was quick work, but the time was short, and I had to 'hustle'. So we had three brand-new press-owners, under securities of only Rs. 2,000 each, instead of Rs. 17,000. I do not think the Press Act was intended to have a motor car, driven by a lady of nearly seventy, rushed through it in this way, like the proverbial 'coach and horses'. But then it was drawn up by bureaucrats who had no experience of Home Rulers; they were accustomed to revolutionaries, and even passive resisters, but had never met with constitutional fighters for Liberty, who regarded them with amused unconcern and perfect good temper. Before we left, Mr. Horniman (Editor of the *Bombay Chronicle*) and Mr. N. C. Kelkar (Editor of the *Mahratta*) came over from Bombay and Poona to offer help, and each wrote an article for the *New India* of the 21st. As they were already Editors, we thought it was better that Mr. P. K. Telang should assume charge of *New India*, and he promptly filled the gap. He forfeited the security in due course, and another Rs. 10,000 was levied. When I resumed the editorship, Mr. Telang presented the Press to Mr.

Ranga Reddi, who started again with another Rs. 2,000. The magistrate, however, most improperly kept the Rs. 10,000 on various excuses for over a year, but when another magistrate took his place, the money was at once refunded. The long fight with good propaganda had helped Home Rule immensely.

"For when we, the interned, foregathered at Ootacamund (where I had, as President of the Theosophical Society, a little house), a whirlwind broke out, raged up and down the country, stormed over to Britain, Russia, France, America, at several hundred miles an hour. Questions were asked in the House of Commons and in the Viceroy's Legislative Council. Members of Parliament, like the babes in the wood, were snowed under with leaves—of paper. 'Who would have thought,' said a very high official pensively, 'that there would have been such a fuss over an old woman?' Crowds of people and many popular leaders joined the Home Rule League. Meetings were held; resolutions flew about; C. P. Ramaswami Aiyar, Jamnadas Dwarkadas, Congressmen everywhere, fanned the storm and rode it. They preserved perfect order; never a window was broken; never a riot occurred; never a policeman was assaulted; never man, woman or child went to gaol. For three months the vehement agitation continued unbrokenly, without ever breaking a law, and the students who wanted to strike were kept in their schools and colleges and then—came the Declaration of August 20, 1917, that the goal of Great Britain in India was Responsible Government, and an announcement that the Secretary of State for India was coming thither to learn the wishes of the people. To 'obtain a calm atmosphere' the three internees were liberated.

"It was a truly constitutional triumph, won by a United India, and was crowned by the election of the Home Rule President (myself) as President of the National Congress of 1917.

"Mr. Montagu, the Secretary of State, came to India, and travelled with the Viceroy, Lord Chelmsford, all over India, meeting Deputations representing every type of political opinion. The National Congress and the Muslim League and the two Home Rule Leagues presented at Delhi on November 26, 1917, memorials asking for Home Rule. The National Congress and the League were represented by a Joint Deputation from their respective Executives, and the memorial was read by Mr. Surendranath Bannerji. After a careful and argumentative presentation of the Indian case it wound up:

"'We submit that the reforms for which the National Congress and the Muslim League plead, are needed as much in the interests of the good government of the country and the happiness and prosperity of the people as for the legitimate satisfaction of our National self-respect and for a due recognition of India's place among the free and civilized Nations of the Empire and the outside world. Nor are they less necessary to strengthen and solidify the British connection with this ancient land. India has given freely of her love and service to England, and she aspires to attain to her proper place of equality and honor in the Commonwealth of Nations, which are proud to own fidelity to his Imperial Majesty the King-Emperor. If, as has been said, the British Empire is the greatest secular power on earth making for the good of mankind, India is hopeful and confident that she will not be denied what is in every way due to her, especially after this great War of Liberty, in which it has been authoritatively recognised that she has played a distinguished and honorable part.'

"The two Home Rule Leagues were represented by Mr. Tilak and myself respectively, and we also read our memorials. At Madras, the All-India Home Rule League presented Mr. Montagu with a million verified signatures, gathered in the Presidency, and conveyed to him in three or four carts.

"It was the end of a strenuous struggle of three crowded years; to me the end of another stage in twenty-four years of steady labor; to the Congress the end of one stage in its thirty-three years of political efforts for Liberty.

"Thenceforth Liberty's battle entered on another phase."

As President of the National Congress—the gift that had, since its foundation, been regarded as the greatest proof of India's love and of her trust—I sketched the causes of what I had called "the New Spirit in India." These were six in number:

1. The awakening of Asia.

2. Discussions abroad on Alien Rule and Imperial Reconstruction.

3. Loss of belief in the superiority of the White Races.

4. The Awakening of the Merchants.

5. The Awakening of the Women to claim their ancient position.

6. The Awakening of the Masses.

The first was largely due to the Russo-Japanese War and to the English ideas of Liberty already mentioned; Lord Minto, as Viceroy of India recognised that "new aspirations were stirring in the hearts of the people, that they were part of a larger movement common to the whole East, and that it was necessary to satisfy them to a reasonable extent by giving them a larger share in the administration". It is difficult for an English Viceroy, however sympathetic, to realise that India wants not "a larger share in the administration," but Self-Government. Similarly I noticed Lord Chelmsford (the Viceroy) start when, in reading the memorial from the Home Rule League above-mentioned, I quoted Mr. Asquith's words, as to the "intolerable degradation of a foreign yoke," as expressing the feeling of the people of India towards the British rule over their country.

Really, the awakening of India is not only a part of the movement in Asia, stimulated by the aggressiveness of western peoples, but it is also part of that World Movement towards Democracy, which began for the West in the revolt of the American Colonies against the rule of Britain, ending in 1776 in the Independence of the Great Republic of the West, and in the French Revolution of 1789. The invasion of India by the European merchants in the seventeenth century and its fatal results in reducing India to ignorance and to poverty; the self-abnegation of the Samurai of Japan; the fall of the Manchu dynasty in China, followed by a Chinese Republic; the struggle of Persia to free herself from the "spheres of influence" of alien Powers; all these had their share in the awakening of India; and she has seen later the fall of the Russian, German and Austrian Empires, and the growth of Democratic institutions all over Europe.

European statesmen pretended that in the War of 1914 to 1918, they were, as Mr. Asquith said, "fighting for nothing but freedom, and for nothing short of freedom". In the speech just quoted, he was promising to stand by France in her claim for the restoration of Alsace and Lorraine, rent from her after the War of 1870, and he defended her claim because those provinces were suffering "the intolerable degradation of a foreign yoke". India has realised that all the talk about Freedom was only meant for white races, and held no sincere sympathy for the colored peoples, however civilized they might be; that the Empire of Britain meant only the rule of the five white Nations instead of one, over colored races, the exploitation of their mineral resources and of their crops for the benefit of Britain, and their working as subordinates, even as slaves, of the white men who had stolen their lands. Indians began to feel that they were not allowed to have a country of their own, like the other Nations of the world; they began to realise that though they had fought for the Freedom, nay, for the very life of the Empire, they were not to share in that Freedom; they glimpsed before themselves a future of subordination, of inferiority, of unbearable humiliation. They had fought as men, as equals; the danger over, they were to fall back into a "subject race".

Subject to whom? To a white race in whose superiority they had lost belief. First the triumph of Japan, and then the frank brutality and cruelty of the European War, the laying waste of cultivated lands, the bombing from the air of cities full of non-combatants, forced them to see the thin veneer of civilization over the savagery of European War, the slaughter of the defenceless, the destruction of magnificent buildings, the architecture centuries old scattered in fragments over a devastated tract. Nothing is left in India of the superstition "of the superiority of Christendom over Asia". "Gazing from afar at the ghastly heaps of the dead and the hosts of the mutilated, at science turned into devilry and ever inventing new tortures for rending and slaying, Asia may be forgiven for thinking that, on the whole, she prefers her own religions and her own civilizations."

The fourth sign of the New Spirit is very significant, for the merchant class had not, as a rule, concerned itself with politics; its special duty was that of the steward of the National resources, organizing agriculture and industries, accumulating wealth and dispensing it, largely in the form of gifts to education, charity to the poor, and generally among useful public purposes. In the organization of the Nation, the merchant was the typical householder, including men of great wealth who made magnificent donations to temples, schools, colleges, universities, and also small traders who gave handfuls of rice or other food-stuffs for the meals of students, gathering such alms for themselves and their teachers. The normal attitude of the Indian merchant—save where de-nationalized by western competition—is the duty of charity, supremely to religion and to education. The War awakened them to the extent in which the foreign Government of India had alienated her natural resources, allowing them to pass into foreign hands; German industries were closed down, and no help was given for their replacement; Government securities became depreciated, and they were forced to sell them to meet their liabilities; Government paid for their goods in War Bonds instead of cash. They were compelled to realise the disadvantages of foreign rule; moreover the depreciation of Government paper made them doubt the stability of the Government. They also realised that India might be far more self-supporting than she was and might export her surplus, as of old, and they also saw the enormous advantage of Self-Government to a country, when they witnessed the rapid increase of Japanese trade under a Home Government. They also noted how strongly their trade rivals, the European Associations in India, opposed Indian Home Rule, and that their own interests would benefit by it. As Mr. J. W. Root had observed, to give Great Britain

"the control over Indian foreign trade and internal industry that would be secured by a common tariff would be an unpardonable iniquity . . . can it be conceived that were India's fiscal arrangements placed to any considerable extent under the control of British legislators, they would not be regarded with an eye to British interests? Intense jealousy of India is always cropping up in everything affecting fiscal or industrial legislation."

The merchant class began to see that Home Rule would be to them an immense advantage, and this explains why, a little later, they contributed largely to Mr. Gandhi's movement, which they mistakenly supposed would bring Home Rule to India.

The awakening of the Women of India was the fifth great factor in the production of the New Spirit. The Theosophical Society had, by strongly aiding the revival of Hinduism, intensified the repugnance felt by Indian women towards foreign and Christian rule. They resented the education that had led away their husbands and sons from allegiance to their own Hindu faith, and which had also for five or six generations pushed away Indian women from their husbands' sides in the new strange phase of public life, caused by the dominance of the foreigner. The home had been closed against him, but he dominated public life and masculine education; the culture of the men became utterly different from that of the women, and while they closed their home doors against him, he closed against them the interests of the larger life of the Nation. They cherished the names of the glorious women of their race, rulers, poets, ascetics, even warriors, and yearned for the re-winning of the elder world. The ill-usage of Indians abroad, the Indenture system with its dishonoring of Indian women, the partition of Bengal and other matters that touched their religion, led to a striking instance of their antagonism to British Rule, when five hundred highly-born women of Bengal went to congratulate the mother of an Editor, sentenced for sedition, for having given birth to so noble a son. I wrote a little later:

"Deep in the heart of India's daughters arose the Mother's Voice, calling on them to help her to arise, and to be once more mistress in her own household. Indian women, nursed on her old literature, with its wonderful ideals of womanly perfection, could not remain indifferent to the great movement for India's liberty. And during the last few years the hidden fire long burning in their hearts, fire of love to Bhāratamātā, fire of resentment against the lessened influence of the religion which they passionately love, instinctive dislike of the foreigner as ruling in their land, have caused a marvellous awakening. The strength of the Home Rule movement is rendered tenfold greater by the adhesion to it of large numbers of women, who bring to its help the uncalculating heroism, the endurance, the self-sacrifice, of the feminine nature. Our League's best recruits and recruiters are among the women of India, and the women of Madras boast that they marched in procession when the men were stopped, and that their prayers in the Temples set the interned captives free. Home Rule has become so intertwined with religion by the prayers offered up in the great Southern Temples—sacred places of pilgrimage—and spreading from them to Village Temples, and also by its being preached up and down the country by Sādhus and Sannyasins, that it has become in the minds of the women and of the ever-religious masses, inextricably intertwined with religion. That is, in this country, the surest way of winning alike the women of the higher classes and the men and women villagers. And that is why I just said that the two words, 'Home Rule,' have become a Mantram."

The Awakening of the Masses inevitably followed the lead of the English-educated Indians. The Indian peasant and artisan had never troubled much about the proceedings of the Governments of Provinces, Kingdoms or Empires. The freely elected Village Council, as we have seen, managed the village affairs for countless generations; since it had been destroyed all had gone wrong with them. The land they had cultivated to support their village Temple and its priest had been seized by some incomprehensible power, and the village school had vanished. The peasant had to pay cash, instead of a share of the crops, to some usurper, who represented the sacred person of the Indian King. His land rent is raised from time to time by some unknown power. He is punished for innocent acts, and for breaking irrational laws that did not exist in the time of his forefathers. He is tyrannised over by village officials who used to be controlled by the village. His educated countrymen lecture to him on interesting matters touching the village life, and help him to join with his fellows in a movement he finds useful—Co-operation. He may read in the *Quarterly Review*:

"The change of attitude on the part of the peasant coupled with the progress made in organization mainly through the Co-operative propaganda, is the outstanding achievement of the last decade, and at the same time the chief ground for the recent confidence with which agricultural reformers can now face the future."

The submerged classes are also moving, much aided by the Brāhmanas, ashamed of their past indifference, and the monster petition of a million signatures, quickly gathered in favor of Home Rule, mentioned above, shows how the people of the Madras Presidency have been awakened to their need of political liberty.

We have seen how Gopāla Krishna Gokhalé spoke of the stunting of his race under British Rule. The Hon. Mr. Bhupendra Basu had also declared:

"A bureaucratic administration, conducted by an imported agency, and centering all power in its hands and undertaking all responsibility, has acted as a dead weight on the Soul of India, stifling in us all sense of initiative for the lack of which we are condemned, atrophying the nerves of action, and, what is most serious, necessarily dwarfing in us all feeling of self-respect."

The cry for Home Rule, Swarāj (Self-Rule), ringing from all parts of India, is really a cry for that which is most priceless in a Nation's life, for the life of its very Soul, for its right to grow, to evolve, on its own National lines. It is an echo of the words:

"What shall it profit a man if he gain the whole world and lose his own Soul? What shall a man give in exchange for his Soul?"

India's very Soul is in peril. The fact that she can deal with her own needs better than Englishmen can deal with them is seen in the action of her only partially free Legislatures since 1921, in giving Free Primary Education to her people, compensation for injury to her factory workers, and the suffrage to her women on the same terms as it is given to men by the Reform Act of 1919.

The Breaking up of United India

A very violent movement led by Lord Sydenham and others, called "The Indo-British Association," arose in Great Britain in 1918, and assisted by the bureaucracy in India, did all that greed of power could do to prevent the Secretary of State for India from proposing effective Reforms. When the Home

Rule Leagues for India sent Deputations to England to work in favor of a generous and statesmanlike policy, they were stopped at Gibraltar by the War Cabinet, their passports cancelled, and their members held in Gibraltar for six weeks. This was done although both Mr. Tilak and myself, the respective Presidents of the Leagues, had declared that we would use to the utmost whatever Reforms were granted in order to obtain more. Much argument arose in India, some declaring, at a Conference held in the Madras Presidency in May, that they would boycott the new Councils if the Reforms were inadequate, and attacking those who would, even if inadequate, utilise them to the utmost.

I urged this utilisation in the *Commonweal*, and was asked why this question should be raised before the report on the tour of the Viceroy and Mr. Montagu was issued. I answered :

> " Because if, in a natural surge of anger and distrust, on finding the Reforms to be inadequate, persons committed themselves to the policy of boycotting the new Councils, it might be difficult for them to retrace their steps, and Parliament, relieved from the fear of an ' Irish Party ' in the new Councils, would ignore the agitation and sit tight, and pass their inadequate measure. There is such a thing as foresight in political work, and it may be well sometimes to look ahead."

Unfortunately the words proved to be prophetic. The Montagu-Chelmsford Report was published in

1918, and three views were taken in India, the basis of subsequent parties; the "Moderates" accepted it, but urged important amendments; the "Home Rulers" declined to accept them, and urged amendments; the "Extremists" declined them altogether. A Special Congress was held in Bombay on August 31 and September 1, and a compromise was agreed to, declaring the proposed Reforms to be "inadequate, unsatisfactory and disappointing," but resolutions were passed which would make them workable. A Conference of Moderates in October made similar amendments, but did not condemn the Report. The regular Congress meeting in December rejected the Pact made in Bombay by an Extremist majority against the protest of the Home Rulers and a few Moderates. Early in 1919 two Deputations went to London, one from the National Congress and one from the Moderate Conference. In February, 1919, the Home Rule League split in twain, in consequence of Mr. Gandhi starting "passive resistance" against the Rowlatt Act, a movement which I opposed, part of the League supporting him, while the other part supported me. Each part sent a Deputation to England, and both did useful work, co-operating with each other and with the Moderates and with the Deputations from the Muslim League and the Congress, and obtaining large amendments in the proposed Bill; we went before the Joint Committee of the two Houses of Parliament as witnesses, and also held various meetings in England. The Rowlatt Act had been passed in a form which could only be broken by revolutionaries, and it had been decided to break other laws, chosen by a committee, as a protest against it, laws such as those which enforced the printing of the printer's name on all publications. This seemed to me such an absurd proposal, that I declined to accept it. I was prepared to disregard a tyrannical law, which cancelled the ordinary rights of a peaceful citizen, and to suffer whatever penalty was imposed for the breach; but I was not prepared to break innocuous laws which I had hitherto obeyed at the command of a committee.

The passive resistance movement of 1919 had been stopped by Mr. Gandhi, who called it a "Himālayan blunder" when it broke into rioting. But the Non-Co-operation movement was none the less started in April, 1920. The Musalmāns were much disturbed about the Khilāfat and Turkey, and had formed a Khilāfat Committee early in 1920, and Mr. Gandhi suggested, if the Turkish Treaty should be unsatisfactory, that, avoiding all forms of violence, people holding office under Government and Government menial servants should resign. "Non-Co-operation with the Government, free from all things of violence, is the only effective remedy open to the people." A hartal (cessation of all work) was called for by Mr. Gandhi for March 19, and was kept all over India. A National week was fixed for April 6 to 13 (the day of the massacre the year before). All parties were represented, and on April 6 the repeal of the Rowlatt Act was demanded. Mr. Gandhi declared that if it were not repealed before the Reforms were started, the request for "Co-operation would be futile, and he, for one, would find the situation such as to make remaining within the Empire impossible" (*New India,* April 7). April 9 was Khilāfat Day, and a resolution was passed that if the just demands of the Musalmāns were not agreed to,

"it will be the duty of every Indian to withdraw Co-operation from Government until pledges are fulfilled and Muslim sentiment conciliated".

A great demonstration was held on April 17 in Madras, and Mr. Gandhi's "four progressive steps" in Non-Co-operation were passed as follows:

"In consonance with the spirit of the Resolution adopted by the All-India Khilāfat Committee, this Conference, in the events of the present agitation proving futile and ineffective, calls upon all Indians to resort to progressive abstention from Co-operation with Government in the following manner:—

"Firstly, to renounce all honorary posts, titles and memberships of Legislative Councils.

"Secondly, to give up all remuneratory posts under Government service.

"Thirdly, to give up all appointments in the Police and Military forces.

"Fourthly, to refuse to pay taxes to Government."

Moulāna Shaukat Ali, after reciting these, as President of the Conference, said:

"We do not embark on this step without fully realising what it means. It means a movement for absolute independence."

Mr. Gandhi did not endorse this, but some of us realised that Non-Co-operation was not a movement for Home Rule as a Free Nation among other Free Nations, with the British Crown as the link of the Federation, but was one of Mass Direct Action, directly revolutionary. As, personally, I regarded the union between India and Great Britain as the one great defence against a war of the white and colored races, I kept up a definite opposition to the Non-Co-operation movement.

The part of the old Home Rule League, which rejected me as President in 1919 in favor of Mr. Gandhi, had accepted a new Constitution from Mr. Gandhi, and became the Swarāj League, a part of the Non-Co-operation movement. The Swarājists boycotted the Legislatures. H.R.H. the Duke of Connaught came to India to open the three Presidency and the Central Legislatures. Both he and the Viceroy declared that autocracy was abandoned, and the King's message proclaimed "the beginning of Swarāj within my Empire". Both King and Duke expressed "their sorrow for the Panjāb tragedy and their sympathy with the sufferers. The Duke's words were broken by strong emotion, moved the whole great Assembly and have rung round India."

The Central Legislature opened well by the Government giving way to the Hon. Mr. V. S. Srinivāsa Sastri, who "moved a resolution accepted by the Government, to examine the Repressive Laws on the Statute Book and report on their repeal or amendment. (The 'Repressive Laws' are those which substitute Executive for Judicial action, and since 1804 have been used arbitrarily to repress political efforts for Reform, placing liberty and property at the mercy of the Executive.) In the Assembly, following up this resolution, Mr. O'Donnell moved and carried a resolution for a committee to examine and report on the Press Laws". Under these fell fourteen Acts dealing with Repression, and three under Press Laws. In the first set twelve and a half Acts were repealed at once, the remaining one and a half to be repealed when the country was less disturbed. In the second, only an amended Registration Act was left.

The first working day in the Assembly was given

"to a resolution moved by Mr. Jamnadas Dwarkadas and accepted by the Government, that expressed regret for the unnecessary humiliations and hardships inflicted on Indians in the Panjāb tragedy, asserted the equality of Indians and Europeans in the sanctity of life and honor, stated some of the punishments inflicted on guilty officers, and promised liberal compensation to families which had suffered in the Jallianwalla Bagh massacre, on a scale similar to that awarded to the British victims. General Dyer had been removed from the Indian Army . . . 1,700 condemned prisoners were released out of 1,786; a political reformer who had been condemned to an extravagant sentence of transportation and confiscation is now (1922) an honored Minister in the Panjāb; the administration of Martial Law was reformed so that no such excesses could happen again, as was proved during the Malabar Rebellion in 1921, 1922."

Other signs of the changed spirit, that it would take too long to recount, were also shown in the various Legislatures, and much useful work was done. I wrote in 1922 on these things, and concluded the recital by paying tribute to those English rulers who had worked for us so well :

" It only needs a little patience and courage on the part of India to win Home Rule through the Reform Act, and Mr. Montagu, as Secretary of State, will remain glorious in Indian History, as the man who opened the gate of the road leading to Home Rule, and stood firmly by India as she began to tread it. Nor should the Viceroy, Lord Chelmsford, be forgotten, who worked with Mr. Montagu through the initial stages, and had the courage to declare at the opening of the Indian Legislature that 'autocracy was abandoned,' laying down, by his own work and will the mighty power he had wielded over more than three hundred millions of human beings. Few are the autocrats, who, like Lord Chelmsford and Mr. Montagu, being offered a great opportunity, have risen to the height of renunciation to which they attained, and, without the compulsion of Revolution, laid at the feet of a great subject Nation the splendid gift of Freedom to tread the path which led to Home Rule, working out her own salvation. The nobility of their action is not yet appreciated, for we are still struggling to reach our goal, and do but poor justice to those who have brought us within reach of it ; we wanted more than they were able to obtain for us, facing the tremendous forces of race pride, consciousness of armed strength, contempt of oriental peoples, and the strong ground of possession unchallenged effectively for one hundred and sixty years, and all the wealth obtained by India's subjection. Against all these they struggled gallantly, and when India rules herself, she will do them justice and gratefully acknowledge the debt she owes them. History will write their names in golden letters, who found a Nation enslaved and set it free to win, by its own strength, its place among the Self-Governing Nations of the world. Never before has so great a Revolution been accomplished without bloodshed ; never before has the autocrat voluntarily resigned power into the hands of subjects, re-created into citizens."

These hopes were frustrated for the time by the success of the Non-Co-operation movement, which not only ruined thousands of school and college students by calling them away from education and then leaving them stranded, but also swept the country under a new tyranny, that of the Swarāj Party, which hooted off the platform those of us who opposed Mr. Gandhi and blocked for the time all political action save obstruction. As I said during that unhappy period :

" Under the Gandhi Rāj there is no Free Speech, no open meeting except for Non-Co-operators. Social and religious boycott, threats of personal violence, spitting, insults in the streets, are the methods of oppression. Mob support is obtained by wild promises, such as the immediate coming of Swarāj, when there will be no rents, no taxes, by giving to Mr. Gandhi high religious names, such as Mahātmā and Avatāra, assigning to him supernatural powers and the like."

Mr. Gandhi never approved of violence, but he could not control his followers, and the result has been a great set-back of Political Reform. Mr. Gandhi's book, *Indian Home Rule,* is full of the wildest statements. At last he called for millions of volunteers and bade people pay no taxes, whereon the Government arrested him, very courteously, and sent him to prison. He said, very truly, that he could not control the forces he had raised. His real followers are non-violent and harmless, for they are now told not to break laws but only to spin and weave.

The National Congress of 1920 at Delhi had carried a resolution demanding (1) that the principle of Self-Determination should be applied to India ; (2) asked for the removal of all hindrances to free discussion ; (3) demanded an Act of Parliament establishing complete responsible Government in India, and that in the reconstruction of Imperial policy (4) India should be placed on an equality with the Self-Governing Dominions. The second point has been almost carried out ; the third and fourth have not. But the Commonwealth of India Bill, as may be seen by referring to the Appendix, will carry them out when it becomes an Act. It has been delayed by the breaking up of political parties caused by the Non-Co-operation movement, now dead.

Shall India become an isolated country or be a Free Nation in a Commonwealth of Free Nations linked together by the British Crown ? My own hope is to see an Indo-British Commonwealth of Colored and White Nations, as otherwise the "clash of color" may cause a fearful war, in which the present civilization will go down as other civilizations before it have gone down. Consider the position as to the ownership of land and the growth of population, as it arises between the Colored and the White Races ; here are some startling figures :

The population of the world is put at 1,800,000,000. Japan and China contain about 500,000,000 ; India and Burma 320,000,000. The rest of Asia south-east of Burma has populations which bring up the total of Asia to nearly 1,000,000,000. And they are all awake, the students in the colleges are full of great ideals, and books are circulating with enormous rapidity, stirring these students to new ambitions.

On the other side of the Pacific and to the South are huge countries sparsely inhabited ; Canada, with an area equal to Europe, has a population of 8,000,000. The United States has 3,000,000 square miles of territory and a population of 105,000,000. Australia has a territory the same as that of the United States and a population of 5,500,000. New Zealand, about the size of the British Isles, has a population of something over 1,000,000. China has territory half as spacious as that of the United States, and over 400,000,000 inhabitants. Let anyone visualise these facts, and ask himself what must be the inevitable issue. The author of the vividly written *The Clash of Colour*, from which these figures are taken, sees "a broad fluttering tide of human beings in Asia pressed by the urgent drive of their own incredible multitude eastward and southward towards the other shores of the Pacific—the relatively sparsely populated lands of America and the open spaces of Australasia." This is not a movement of war but of economic compulsion, an inevitable irresistible movement of the hungry towards the empty fertile lands where Nature will reward labor with food. If resisted by legislation, it will burst into war, war implacable and sustained. Once the struggle blazes into war, numbers must tell. "In the clash of arms, laws are silent." And such a war will not end before the present civilization has received its death-blow.

But if India and Britain come to terms, if India becomes an equal partner in the firm instead of a servant, then all will be changed. As Mr. Rushbrook Williams says, in one of his masterly reports, *India in* 1922-23:

"The impending struggle between East and West, foretold by many persons who cannot be classed either as visionaries or as fanatics, may easily be mitigated or even entirely averted, if the British Commonwealth of Nations can find a place within its wide compass for three hundred and twenty millions of Asiatics, fully enjoying the privileges, and adequately discharging the responsibilities, which at present characterise the inhabitants of Great Britain and the Self-Governing Dominions."

If India be fully admitted into the Commonwealth of Nations, if she possesses Dominion status at Home as well as abroad, then may a World Peace brood over our seething Nations. In 1919 I urged that India should determine for herself her own form of Self-Government, and reference to the Appendix will show how that idea has been carried out in the Commonwealth of India Bill, now before the House of Commons.

The Future of India will, I hope, be united with that of Britain for the sake of both Nations and for the sake of Humanity at large, for they supply each other's defects, and united can do for the world a service that neither can do alone. India in the Past has shown that the highest spirituality does not prevent, but ensures, the greatness of achievement in the many-aspected splendor of a Nation's life; under the shelter of her sublime religion she developed a literature of unparalleled intellectual power, philosophical and metaphysical; her Art flowered into exquisite beauty; her dramas still purify and inspire. Her physical prosperity endured millennium after millennium, and her wealth was the envy of the world. Let her have Freedom to develop on her own lines and she will again rival her ancient glory, and even excel it in the future. Robbed of Liberty, she is treading the path of death, and will soon leave the world only the memory of what she was. Critical are the coming years, wherein the decision must be made.

Let India remember what she was and realise what she may be. Then shall her Sun rise once more in the East and fill the western lands with Light.

Her salvation lies in Swarāj, Self-Rule, Home Rule, and in that alone. Nothing else can preserve and renew her vitality—slowly ebbing away before our eyes. Yet that vitality has endured from a Past for which archæological research has not as yet discovered a boundary, beyond which the Mother-Race of the present civilized Nations of the world did not raise her stately head, wearing the aureole of spiritual glory, holding her sceptre of intellectual and moral achievement over the countless millions of her children, spreading westwards ever till their setting Sun becomes the Rising Sun on their ancient ancestral Homeland.

PEACE TO ALL BEINGS

APPENDIX

APPENDIX

THE COMMONWEALTH OF INDIA BILL

THIS Bill was not a sudden move, but was led up to by progressive steps.

In September, 1913, a small band of my immediate Theosophical workers formed themselves into a group called "The Brothers of Service" to prepare for steady advance not only along the lines named above of Religious, Educational and Social Reform, but also along Political, since the intolerable pressure of tyrannical legislation hampered all forward action. They drew up the following leaflet which was widely circulated:

> "'Theosophy must be made practical' was a sentence written and published long ago by one of Those whom Theosophists regard as Masters. Since Mrs. Annie Besant came to India in 1893, she has been seeking for ways of service to India, so that the country of her adoption might rise in the scale of Nations, and take the world-position to which her past entitles her and which her future will justify. Rightly or wrongly, she judged that the great Forward Movement must begin with a revival of spirituality, for National self-respect could only be aroused and the headlong rush towards imitation of western methods could only be checked, by substituting spirituality and idealism for materialism. Great success attended the work, and she then added to it educational activities, so as to appeal to the citizens of the future and shape their aspirations towards Nationhood, as an integral part of the coming World-Empire. Cautiously she carried on some Social Reform activities, organizing propaganda against child-marriage, and in favour of foreign travel, helping the latter by the establishment of an Indian Hostel in London,* and of a Committee of friendly Theosophists who would welcome youths arriving in England as strangers. For many years many of her more attached

* This is an error; we only kept a register of lodging-houses with trustworthy landladies, and of private families where Indian lads would be taken as paying guests.

followers have been pledged to delay the marrying of their children for some years beyond the custom of their caste and neighborhood. In Politics, she has urged the larger ideals, and has, especially in England, spoken for the just claims of India.

"Believing that the best interests of India lie in her rising into ordered freedom under the British Crown, in the casting away of every custom which prevents union among all who dwell within her borders, and in the restoration to Hinduism of social flexibility and brotherly feeling,

I PROMISE:

"1. To disregard all restrictions based on Caste.

"2. Not to marry my sons while they are still minors, nor my daughters till they have entered their seventeenth year. ('Marry' includes any ceremony which widows one party on the death of the other.)

"3. To educate my wife and daughters—and the other women of my family, so far as they will permit—to promote girls' education, and to discountenance the seclusion of women.

"4. To promote the education of the masses as far as lies in my power.

"5. To ignore all color distinctions in social and political life, and to do what I can to promote the free entry of colored races into all countries on the same footing as white immigrants.

"6. To oppose actively any social ostracism of widows who remarry.

"7. To promote union among the workers in the fields of spiritual, educational, social and political progress, under the headship and direction of the Indian National Congress."

It was further pointed out that while the Theosophical Society could not, *as a whole*, be committed to special lines of activities, it should work in India as it was doing in England, "ventilating plans for profound social re-organization with love instead of hatred as an inspiration. She (Mrs. Besant) aims at the ever-closer union of the British and Indian races by mutual understanding and mutual respect". A further publication urged "the changes necessary to enable her (India) to take her equal place among the Self-Governing Nations which owe allegiance to the British crown". Religious Hindus were warmly invited to join in the work, "in order that they may preserve to India the ancient and priceless religion of Hinduism, now threatened with decay by its practical separation from the movement of Progress in India". It was stated that Hinduism should shelter all progressive movements, and not stand apart in selfish isolation. "Let her cling only to the essentials—the Immanence of God and the Solidarity of Man. All gracious customs and elevating traditions may be followed by her children, but not imposed on the unwilling, nor used as barriers to prevent social union. So shall she become a unifier instead of a divider, and again assert her glory as the most liberal of religions, the model of an active spirituality, which inspires intellectual vigor, moral purity and national prosperity."

This was followed by a course of lectures delivered by me in Madras, in October and November, 1913, the subjects of which show how definitely the Reform Movement was guided, and the chairmen the type of men who supported it.

Foreign Travel: Chairman, Dr. S. Subramania Iyer, late Acting Chief Justice of the Madras High Court.

Child-Marriage and Its Results: Chairman, the Hon. Dewan Bahadur T. S. Sadasiva Iyer, M.L., Acting Judge of the Madras High Court.

Our Duty to the Depressed Classes: Chairman, the Hon. Justice B. Tyabji.

Indian Industries as Related to Self-Government: Chairman, Dewan Bahadur M. Ādinārāyana Iyah.

Appendix to the above lecture.

1. Exports.
2. Weaving.
3. Political Effects.
4. Moral Effects.

Mass Education: Chairman, the Hon. Justice Miller.

The Education of Indian Girls: Chairman, the Hon. Mr.

P. S. Sivaswāmi Aiyer, C.I.E., C.S.I., Indian Member of the Executive Council, Madras.

The Color Bar in England, the Colonies and India: Chairman, the Hon. Mr. Kesava Pillai.

The Passing of the Caste System: Chairman, Dewan Bahadur L. A. Govindarāghava Iyer.

It will be noticed that the three first Chairmen were Judges of the High Court, two (Theosophist) Hindus and one Musalmān, while an English Judge was the Chairman of the fifth lecture. The eighth was also a Theosophist. All the lectures dealt with burning social questions, and were intended to lead up to a Political Movement.

With the object of training ourselves in Parliamentary methods, on January 1, 1915, it was proposed to form a "Madras Parliament," a Debating Society with Parliamentary forms. We passed a Pañchayat Act, presented by Mr. T. Rangachari, now a member of the Legislative Assembly and its late Deputy President; an Education Act, presented by Mr. C. P. Ramaswami Aiyar, now Law Member, Vice-President of the Madras Executive Council, K.C.I.E.; and a Commonwealth of India Act presented by myself, the parent of the Bill now before the House of Commons. We flooded the country with pamphlets, bearing the stirring motto:

"We bring the Light that saves:
We bring the Morning Star:
Freedom's good things we bring you,
Whence all good things are."

Another series, *New India* Political Pamphlets, had the motto:

"How long ere thou take station?
How long ere thralls live free?"

How India Wrought for Freedom, the story of the Congress from 1885 to 1914, was published week by week in the *Commonweal*, and was published as a book with a Historical Preface, arousing great wrath in the I.C.S. and the Anglo-Indian press, being a narrative of facts, then known to few, but now used by writers on India, and familiar all over the country. In *New India* we wrote on grievances, demanded Home Rule, hammered away day in and day out. " Home Rule " was woven into scarves, borders of saris, handkerchiefs. Its red and green colors appeared everywhere. Then we decided to have a Home Rule League, and Mr. Dadabbai Naorogi approved, but the local leaders were more cautious, fearing it might weaken the Congress, whereas we wanted to carry on a continuous agitation to support Congress in the equality it had claimed in the Congress of 1914. The effect of the agitation, aided by the before quoted words of Asquith, and the daily news from fields of battle, swept over the land, carrying all before it. Here are two extracts, a prose one and a song of my own writing, which show the feeling of those thrilling days:

" While this many-featured and powerful educational agitation—a thoroughly healthy and constitutional one, never once disfigured by violence—was going on all over the country, the circumstances of the time were such as to force the Nation rapidly forward into a consciousness of Nationhood, and of her then place in the eyes of the world, a place so unworthy of her storied past, and of the virility of her people in the present, when stirred by a call that moved them to exertion. That call came from the War, which became more and more terrible as it swept over the lands, and India became full of pride in the prowess of her soldiers, fighting side by side with the flower of European troops, and fighting against the mightiest army in the world. India felt herself living as her children died for Freedom, and the villages which sent their men became conscious of a wider and more stirring world. The words of English statesmen, spoken to enhearten their own countrymen, rang across the seas to India. Asquith spoke of what England would feel if Germans filled her highest offices, controlled her policy, levied her taxes, made her laws; it would be inconceivable, he cried, and intolerable. India listened, and murmured to herself: 'But that is exactly my condition; here, these same Englishmen think it the only conceivable and the only tolerable life for me.' He spoke of the 'intolerable degradation of a foreign yoke'; India whispered: 'Is it so? Do Englishmen think thus? What, then, of me?' She had accepted English rule by habit; now she was shocked into realising the position which she filled in the eyes of the world. A subject Nation. A subject race. Was that really how the white Nations looked on her? Was that why her sons were treated as coolies in the outside world? Did a foreign yôke at home mean unspeakable humiliations abroad?

"Then the pride of the Aryan Motherland awoke. Had she not a civilisation dating back by millennia, beside which these white races, sprung from her womb, were but of yesterday? Had she not been rich, strong, and self-ruled, while these wandered naked in their forests, and quarrelled with each other? Had she not lived as equal with the mightiest Nations of a far-off past, when Babylon was the wonder of the world, when the streets of Nineveh were crowded, when Egypt was the teacher of wisdom, when Persia was a mighty Empire, when Greek philosophy was an offshoot of her schools, when Rome clad her haughtiest matrons in the products of her looms? Had not many a Nation invaded her, and had she not either driven them back, or assimilated them, and re-created them into Indians? Had not the gold of the world flowed into her coffers? Yet now she was poor. Had not great Empires, now dead, sent ambassadors to her Courts? But now she was 'a Dependency' of a little far-off Island in northern seas. She had been asleep. She had been dreaming. But now she awakened. She opened her eyes, and looked around her. She saw her peasants, starving at home, but holding their own as soldiers abroad. The coolies, despised in England's Colonies, were cheered as heroes by Englishmen in the streets of their capital city. Yes, Asquith was right: 'the intolerable degradation of a foreign yoke.' If she was worthy to fight for Freedom, she was worthy to enjoy it. If she stood equal with Englishmen, Scotchmen, Colonials, in the trenches, and her poured-out blood mingled with theirs, indistinguishably soaking into French and Flemish soil, then she should be equal with them in her own ancient land. The souls of her dead in France, in Belgium, in Gallipoli, in Palestine, in Syria, in Mesopotamia, in East Africa, cried to her to claim the Freedom for which their bodies lay scattered far from home and kin. India sprang to her feet—a Nation.

"And then, because a white woman had been crying in her sleeping ears these truths about herself for more than twenty years, and was crying them aloud still in her ears awakened by the crash of War, she turned to her for a while as her natural leader, who had blown the conch for Liberty's battle in India. And she sang!"

Here is one of the songs:

"WAKE UP, INDIA

"Hark! the tramp of marching numbers,
India, waking from her slumbers,
Calls us to the fray.
Not with weapons slaughter dealing,
Not with blood her triumph sealing,
But with peace-bells loudly pealing,
Dawns her Freedom's Day.

"Justice is her buckler stainless,
Argument her rapier painless,
Truth her pointed lance.
Hark! her song to Heaven ringing,
Hatreds all behind her flinging,
Peace and joy to all she's bringing,
Love her shining glance.

'Mother, Dear! all victorious,
Thou hast seen a vision glorious,
Dreamt of Liberty.
Now the vision has its ending
In the truth, all dreams transcending,
Hope and fact together blending,
Free! from sea to sea.

"By thy plains and snow-clad mountains,
By thy streams and rushing fountains,
By Himalayan heights,
By the past of splendid story,
By the hopes of future glory,
By the strength of wisdom hoary,
Claim thy sacred Rights."

And she claimed them.

The Commonwealth of India Bill.

We all considered it vital that the Indian Constitution should be framed by Indians, and in answer to a question from Lord Selborne—the Chairman of the Joint Committee of the Houses of

Lords and Commons in 1919, addressed to myself as witness—whether India would ever be satisfied with a Constitution drawn up by Englishmen, I replied in the negative, basing the reply on the great age of her civilisation and the difference of manners and customs.

The practical framing of a Constitution for India by Indians took birth in February, 1922, in a discussion in the Political Section of the 1921 Club, Madras, on the method of winning Swarāj. Mr. V. S. Rāmaswami Sāstri, then Assistant Editor of *New India*, the brother of the Rt. Hon. V. S. Srinivāsa Sāstri, P.C., suggested that India should resort to a Convention for the framing of a Constitution. The idea was adopted and discussed widely in the press. The Political Section sent Dr. Annie Besant to Simla in September, where the Indian Legislature was in session, to seek its views; informal meetings were held by members of each House separately, and both approving the idea of calling a Convention, a joint meeting was held which elected an Executive Committee from among themselves to call a Conference of members of the Central and Provincial Legislatures to arrange and call a Convention. The Conference met in February, 1923, at Delhi, during the session of the Indian Legislature, and after some days' discussion, outlined the essentials of a Constitution carrying out the resolution of the Congress of 1918 to place India on an equality with the Self-Governing Dominions of the British Empire. The Conference Executive drew up a pledge for candidates for the Legislatures at the forthcoming elections in the autumn, accepting the outline and binding them to call the Convention. This was done, and a second Conference met in February, 1924. This approved the work of the year 1923, and called the Convention, into which it then merged itself, to meet in April, 1924. It consisted of Members and ex-Members of the Legislatures, Central and Provincial (231), the members of the Council of the National Home Rule League (19), the elected representatives of the Political Sections of the 1921 Clubs in Madras, Bombay and Calicut (3), the co-opted representatives of the Indian Women's Association (2), and the late Law Member of the Governor-General's Council, 256 in all, and this Convention is responsible for the Commonwealth of India Bill. Until now, every member has been an elected representative, all but a handful belonging to the elected Members of the Legislatures.

It divided itself into seven Committees to deal with different

Sections of a Constitution establishing Self-Government, and directed them to report in the autumn of the same year. A draft was based on these reports, and the Convention sat in Bombay in December and considered and amended it. It printed the results and circulated them to political parties inviting further amendments, and submitted the draft also to a sub-committee appointed by a Committee of all parties, presided over by Mr. Gandhi in November, 1924. This sub-committee made a number of amendments, and these with all others were submitted to the Convention sitting in Cawnpur on April 11, 12 and 13, 1925; it was finally submitted to a Drafting Committee in Madras, consisting of the Hon. Mr. C. P. Rāmaswāmi Aiyar, Messrs. Shiva Rao, Sri Rām, Yādunandan Prasād and Dr. Annie Besant, with power to correct any oversights in language where necessary, to see the Bill through the press, and publish it in the name of the Convention.

In May, 1925, it was sent to England to Major D. Graham Pole, the Hon. Secretary of the British Committee on Indian Affairs. He laid it before leading members of the Labor Party and it was backed by them, read a first time in the House of Commons and ordered to be printed. It then went before the Executive Committee of the Parliamentary Labor Party, that examines every Bill before it is taken up by the Labor Government or Opposition, as the case may be. It was closely examined, clause by clause, and finally passed unanimously as embodying the resolutions passed by the Labor Party from time to time respecting India. It thus passed into the hands of the future Labor Government, and was put on the list of bills balloted for as an official measure.

SUMMARY OF BILL.

General Principles.

India will be placed on an equal footing with the Self-Governing Dominions, sharing their responsibilities and their privileges.

The right of Self-Government will be exercised from the Village upwards in each successive autonomous area of wider extent, namely, the Taluka; the District; the Province; and India (excluding the Indian States).

The three great spheres of activity, Legislative, Executive and Judicial, will, as far as possible, be independent of each other, while correlated in their working.

Declaration of Rights.

The following Fundamental Rights will be guaranteed to every person: (*a*) Inviolability of the liberty of the person and of his dwelling and property, save by process of law in a duly constituted Court of Law. (*b*) Freedom of conscience and the free practice of religion, subject to public order or morality. (*c*) Free expression of opinion and the right of assembly peaceably and without arms, and of forming Associations or Unions, subject to public order or morality. (*d*) Free Elementary Education as soon as practicable. (*e*) The use of roads, places dedicated to the public, Courts of Justice and the like. (*f*) Equality before the law, irrespective of considerations of Nationality, and (*g*) Equality of sexes.

Legislative.

Legislative power is vested in the King, a Legislative Assembly and a Senate. "Parliament" shall mean only the Parliament of the Commonwealth of India. The Legislative Assembly will consist of 300 Members, and the Senate of 150.

The Senate will have equal powers with the Legislative Assembly except in regard to Money Bills, which will originate only in the latter. The life of the Legislative Assembly will ordinarily be for five years, that of the Senate for six years. The Senate will have a continuous existence, with half the number of Members retiring every three years by a process of rotation.

In the Provincial Legislative Councils, the number of Members will vary from 100 to 200 according to the size and importance of the Province. The life of a Legislative Council will ordinarily be for four years. There will be at present only one Chamber in a Provincial Legislature, but provision has been made in the Bill for the addition of a Second Chamber in a Province, if it so decides.

In the District, Taluka, and Village Councils, which are termed the Sub-Provincial Units of Government, the number of members will vary according to local conditions. The ordinary life-term of the District Councils will be for three years, that of the Taluka for two years, and that of the Village Councils for one year.

Franchises.

The franchises for the various Legislative bodies have been graded, commencing with universal adult suffrage in the Village, and restricted by higher educative, or administrative, or property or other monetary qualifications in the case of each higher body.

The principle of direct election has been maintained throughout, except in the case of the Senate, where candidates will be nominated to a panel from which the electorate will make its choice. A distinction has also been observed between Members and Electors, the qualifications for the former being kept at a somewhat higher level than for the latter.

The powers of the various Legislative bodies have been embodied in a Schedule to the Constitution; and residuary powers have been vested in the Parliament.

Defence.

There will be a Defence Commission with a majority of Indians thereon, every five years, appointed by the Viceroy in consultation with his Cabinet. The Commission will recommend a minimum of non-votable expenditure for the Defence Forces and also report on the progress of the Indianisation of those Forces. In the event of disagreement, the Viceroy will have power to secure the minimum which, in his opinion, is necessary for the Defence Forces. No revenue of India may be spent on any branch of Defence Forces in which Indians are ineligible for holding commissioned rank. As soon as the Commission recommends favorably, Parliament may pass an Act to undertake the full responsibility of Defence.

Executive.

There will be a Cabinet in the Government of India consisting of the Prime Minister and not less than seven Ministers of State, who will be collectively responsible for the administration of the Commonwealth. The Prime Minister will be appointed by the Viceroy, and the other Ministers on the nomination of the Prime Minister. The Viceroy will be *temporarily* in charge of the Defence Forces. In all matters except Defence, the Viceroy will act only upon the advice of the Cabinet. The salaries of the Viceroy and of the Members of the Cabinet will be fixed by Parliament, but in the case of the former, no alteration will come into force during his continuance in office. The Cabinet will resign as soon as it has lost the support of a majority in the Legislative Assembly.

In the Provinces, the same principles will apply as in the Central Government, except that the minimum number of Ministers will be three.

The Secretary of State.

The powers and functions of the Secretary of State and the Secretary of State in Council over the revenues and the administration of India will be transferred to the Commonwealth Executive.

Judicial.

There will be a Supreme Court of India, consisting of a Chief Justice and not less than two other Judges with original as well as appellate jurisdiction to deal with such matters as may be determined by statute. It will have power to deal with all matters arising out of the interpretation of the Constitution or of laws made by the Parliament. It will also be the final appellate authority in India, unless it certifies that the question is one which should be determined by the Privy Council.

The existing High Courts will have the same powers and authority as before the establishment of the Commonwealth.

Finance.

The revenues of Parliament will form a consolidated revenue fund, and will be vested in the Viceroy. No revenue may be raised by the Executive without the sanction of Parliament.

The allocation of revenues between Parliament and the Provinces will be decided by a Finance Commission every five years.

New Provinces.

Parliament will have the power to alter the limits of existing Provinces or establish new Provinces and make laws for their administration.

Minorities.

Communal Representation as now existing will be abolished, and all elections will be held on the basis of purely territorial electorates. As a temporary measure, the number of seats now reserved for Musalmāns and Europeans will be guaranteed for five years, at the end of which period the question of its continuance, modification or abolition will be examined by a Franchise Commission.

Bills affecting the religion or the religious rites or usages of a community or communities will be referred to a Standing Committee of the Legislature in which they are introduced; and if the Committee, on which there will be a majority of the members of the community or communities concerned, reports adversely, such Bills will lapse for the period of one year.

Public Services.

There will be a Public Services Commission to exercise full control over the public services of India as regards recruitment, discipline, promotion and pensions. Officers now in the service of the Government of India or of the Provincial Governments will be guaranteed their existing rights but, at the establishment of the Commonwealth, they will pass into the service of the Commonwealth or the Provinces, as the case may be.

Alteration of the Constitution.

Parliament will have power to alter the Constitution.

The Schedules.

The First Schedule gives the oath of allegiance and affirmation to His Majesty King George V and his heirs and successors.

The Second Schedule—

(1) Electors must be at least 21 years of age.

(2) Qualifications for the graded electorates are given, beginning with the Village, where universal suffrage is provided for. The qualifications of the remaining electorates relate to (*a*) administrative experience, (*b*) education—literary or technical, (*c*) economic and industrial ministration (co-operative stores and banks, wells, tanks and canals, cottage industries, forests, local taxation, works of public utility), (*d*) income, (*e*) possession of land property, (*f*) occupation of a house; thus including different classes of citizens. These qualifications are graded, being very low for the Taluka (collection of villages), and highest for the Senate. Only *one* of the varions qualifications is required to qualify a man or woman as a voter in any council.

The Third Schedule.

The powers of each Council, from the Village Pañchayat to the Parliament, are fully stated.

The Fourth Schedule.

(1) There will be no communal electorates, but as a transitory provision, the same number of seats will be reserved for Musalmāns as is provided for in the Government of India Act, 1918, for five years, when a Franchise Commission will report on its continuance, amendment or abolition.

(2) Proposed legislation affecting religions shall be postponed for one year if a Committee of the House in which the legislation is introduced, and consisting of a majority of members of the religion or religions affected, decide against the measure.

(3) The number of members assigned to the Provinces for the various legislative bodies are given.

(4) The salaries of the Viceroy, Governors and the Commonwealth and Provincial Ministers are given.